Pigeon
Advanced

Pigeon Racing
Advanced Techniques

by

JAN AERTS

Translated by Inge Moore

faber and faber
LONDON · BOSTON

First published in 1969
by Faber and Faber limited
3 Queen Square London WC1N 3AU
Reissued 1973
First published in Faber Paperbacks 1981
Reprinted 1987
Printed in Great Britain by
Redwood Burn Limited, Trowbridge, Wiltshire

All rights reserved

© "La Paloma" Buchverlag u.–Vertrieb
Hamburg 52 (Hochkamp)
English translation © 1969 Faber and Faber Ltd

This book is sold subject to the condition that is shall not, by way of trade or otherwise, be lent, resold, hired out or otherwise circulated without the publisher's consent in any form of binding or cover other than that in which it is published and without a similar condition including this condition being imposed on the subsequent purchaser.

British Library Cataloguing in Publication Data

Aerts, Jan
Pigeon racing.
1. Pigeon racing
798'.8 SF469

ISBN 0–571–11572–1

To Marguerite, my dear wife, whose inexhaustible patience with me as a pigeon fancier and as an author, made so much possible

and

To Leon F. Whitney, D.V.M., in appreciation of his scientific help, and his wife Catherine, for her unforgettable hospitality in Orange, Connecticut, U.S.A.

Contents

Foreword	*page* 11
1. The fancier, his qualifications for success and dependence on others	15
2. The selection of breeding stock	33
3. The breeding system	55
4. The environment	72
5. The loft	83
6. Feeding	91
7. Racing systems	106
8. The pigeon	115
9. Back from the race	129
10. How do our pigeons find their way home?	143
11. A look behind the scenes	160
12. And finally, a look at Fabry	186

Publisher's Note

The text of this edition follows that of our earlier edition of 1969 since when we are sorry to note that Leon F. Whitney has died

Foreword

Pigeon-fancying is a declining sport today. Many reasons have been put forward, and in the process quite a number of top-ranking fanciers have had the blame laid at their doors. With great enthusiasm and a lot of goodwill, a campaign has now been started to get young people to take up pigeon racing, for they are the ones we must convince if our sport is to survive. What do they have to be convinced of? That young people can get a great deal of fun out of pigeon racing . . . ?

To be quite honest, there is more fun available today in other sports in which young people can become proficient much more quickly and with fewer disappointments. The young people of fifty years ago met by the church on Sundays. Means of transport were primitive, and their pocket money was far from lavish. What was there in the way of amusements? So they raced pigeons or went round to a neighbour to wait for his birds to return home.

As the national income rose gradually so the income of every individual rose with it. Everybody is better off today. Those who do not want to participate actively in a sport can be spectators; they can travel, and explore the countryside. Distances are no longer any object. Anyone can get what he wants for his money.

The fact that fewer and fewer young people take interest in our sport is a logical consequence of this change. But that is only one of several causes. Our sport has become too commercialized.

Foreword

There are many aspects of it these days which have precious little to do with pigeons and which we could well do without.

Modern publicity bombards us with scientific jargon to try to convince us that we cannot breed and race our pigeons or keep them healthy without a virtual 'pigeon pharmacy'. Since we are all gamblers at heart (why not be honest) and optimists into the bargain ('tomorrow things will be better') we fall an easy prey to this kind of persuasion. True, it takes some strength of character to admit that a competitor's success results from his superior knowledge and better pigeons. We try this and that and come to the conclusion that the other chap must be 'giving his birds something'. Why should he be doing so much better? And that's when we start going astray!

I shall have an opportunity later on in the book to talk about a number of other causes, but one thing is certain: if we want to preserve the sport and get more people interested in it as spectators we must clean it up. Our sport could be run in an efficient, cheap and simple way. My long experience, as a fancier and journalist, my daily contact with the country's greatest and most famous breeders, with personalities like Dr. Whitney, Director of the Whitney Veterinary Clinic in New Haven, U.S.A., who is a fancier himself, will help you to develop an objective eye for pigeons and the sport of pigeon racing and to examine critically what I have to say in this book.

My first book *Gij en ik over duiven* (*You and I on Pigeons*) was published in 1948 and ran into four editions. That is quite a while ago now, and time does not stand still.

Like everything else, the sport of pigeon racing is changing all the time, and improving too. We have to go along with progress, otherwise nothing will ever change and certainly nothing will ever improve. The full extent of this progress becomes apparent only when you keep pigeons yourself and get an opportunity to see the best lofts and the best pigeons in the country.

But I am not going to condemn what I have formerly extolled. Principles are unaffected by the passage of time; it is only methods that change. The basic rules in pigeon racing will

Foreword

always be the same. Their application, however, differs from fancier to fancier. Anyone who has been racing his pigeons without success can learn from those who have the know-how. The successful fancier strives after constant improvement; his is a continuous struggle. Though perfection is never attainable, one draws ever closer to it.

I have tried to be uncomplicated and factual throughout the book and to make it intelligible to a breeder on the most modest scale. I hope I have succeeded in this endeavour. It is inevitable that I should have quoted names; I could not do without them. But mine is the full responsibility for all I have written.

In recent years, my library has been enriched by a great number of works on pigeon racing. Foreign magazines and letters from pigeon fanciers in many countries that practise the sport come flooding on to my desk every day. Quite a few fanciers, (and by no means the least-known ones, at that) treat me practically as a member of the family. What is the result? A man who eats, sleeps and thinks pigeons as I do develops a keen eye for a great many things. He learns to differentiate between fact and illusion; he has both feet on the ground and realizes that true and genuine art is at the same time simple art. This applies to pigeon racing, too.

Both to professionals and amateurs our sport is worthwhile only if it is free of all superfluous trimmings, free of 'everything that is irrelevant to pigeons and pigeon racing', as my late friend Louis Vermeijen so rightly said.

1969　　　　　　　　　　　　　　　　　　　　　　　　　Jan Aerts

1

The fancier, his qualifications for success and dependence on others

It is gratifying to notice that more and more fanciers make use of technical literature. An increasing number turn to books to widen their knowledge. Of all the periodicals, those which regularly publish instructive articles, providing their readers with objective reports on the most successful lofts, meet with the greatest response. Of course, they cannot do without race reports during the season, but these take second place. There is still great scope for improvement in pigeon literature, but some progress has undoubtedly been made.

A book on pigeons must be as complete as possible and must deal with all aspects of the sport. In most books one aspect has been completely omitted or dealt with only perfunctorily: I mean the fancier himself; what makes the true sportsman, how he thinks and acts. For this reason I will deal with him first of all.

A fancier who has a brilliant racing record and keeps it up is considered to own good pigeons and to be an expert. Anyone may win a top prize once in a while, and if he does he owes it to good pigeons. Only if he remains at the top for longer than just one or two seasons can we call him an expert. If a fancier acquires some pigeons from a famous loft and gets only a mediocre performance from them, he is said have bought the pigeons but not the breeder. This leads me to the conclusion that the true

The fancier, his qualifications for success

breeder, the expert, must possess certain qualities. True, the pigeons must be good, the loft must meet certain conditions, the food must be scientifically balanced, etc. . . . But the fancier himself remains the most important factor, the centre around which everything revolves. On him depend success or failure.

In my opinion the most important qualities a fancier should possess are:

Patience—Character—An observant eye—The ability to concentrate and to plan.

Patience means much the same as quiet perseverance. It is unimportant how much time is spent on reaching an aim, as long as the aim is reached in the end. Patience is a paramount requirement. I often point this out in my articles in *De Duif*, calling it dogged patience, Benedictine patience. Why 'Benedictine' patience? The Benedictine order of monks is the oldest in the West. The monks used to be occupied mainly with studying and copying old manuscripts. Printing had not then been invented. Everything had to be put on paper with a pen and a brush. In monastery libraries we can still see these massive tomes, beautifully written and filled with artistically ornamented initials. Very often one such book was the work of a single monk. A whole lifetime spent on just one book! If that isn't patience, I don't know what is.

It may not take a lifetime to build up a loft, to breed a strain and to become a recognized fancier, but far too many people expect to become well-known and successful fanciers in no time at all, with a loft that is thrown together and pigeons that only cost a few coppers. Success does not come as quickly as that.

While patience is synonymous with quiet perseverance, *character* is the hallmark of a strongly-developed personality. Patience and character are inseparably linked, complementary qualities. A man with patience and character knows what he wants. He sets himself an aim and he intends to reach it by following a carefully thought-out plan, from which he will not deviate unless experience shows that he has not chosen the best possible way. Then he will admit his mistake and alter his plan. He will *alter* it, not *abandon* it.

The fancier, his qualifications for success

In November 1961 I visited Emile Matterne at his home in Overhespen (Tienen). He is a teacher at the Royal Athenaeum at Malines and a pigeon fancier in his spare time. He is completely dedicated to this hobby. His villa lies just off the main road from Brussels to Liège, screened from the noise by shrubs and poplar trees. The whole of the upper floor has been turned into a pigeon loft and there are more lofts in the garden behind the house. Matterne's occupation does not allow him to take part in short-distance races so he only races over long distances.

A staff member of *De Duif* used my very words in a report headlined: 'National Champion 1961', 'Patience is Rewarded', 'Entire Loft Bred from Famous Pigeons', 'No Missing Link in Building up Strain', 'Pigeons with a Flawless Pedigree', 'Simplicity, Character, and a Massive Dose of Patience'. So my views on what makes the born breeder are shared by others.

I visited Matterne a fortnight after this, and was especially impressed by his method of selection. Young cocks and hens have separate quarters. They are raced from Momignies some sixty miles away. Some hens go as far as Bourges (320 miles), because, after all, Matterne is a long-distance racer. He selects his best birds after the moult. Inevitably, even some of the better birds have to go. Matterne can see no way round this, he just cannot keep them all.

The yearlings are mated and allowed to rear two young in the nest at any one time throughout the year. They are raced over 120 miles on the 'natural' system, i.e. while sitting or rearing youngsters. Why on the natural system? The fancier gets to know his birds; they must be able to keep their weight or they are no good. The actual race results are relatively unimportant. What matters is that with the natural system the birds get well 'run in' and that they moult better. Experience shows that yearlings moult better on the natural system than on widowerhood. The natural system seems to favour their proper physical development. At two years old they go into the basket to be tested on long-distance flights. But not as far as St. Vincent (629

The fancier, his qualifications for success

miles)! Those who pass this final test 'with merit' are suited for their proper task, the difficult long-distance races.

This is his principle of selection, to which he adheres strictly. His results have justified it. (*Muster of Belgium* one year, close to it in other years!)

It takes character and patience to find out what a pigeon can do, what it needs and what its breeder may ask of it. It is the same everywhere, whether over short or long distances. I can quote examples for every specialized field of our sport.

Let us assume, for example, that you pair a cock with a hen to find a good breeding pair. How long will it be before you know whether the experiment has succeeded? I have asked many people this question and hardly ever received the right answer. Many say, 'I'll know when I have trained the young.' Not a chance! A young bird is learning, a yearling goes through a probationary period—it is only when it is two years old that the bird passes its final test. Of course, we are now talking of pigeons which can be judged at sight, which look promising in the beginning and show no faults or weaknesses that would make them unsuitable for racing.

Young birds are usually overtaxed; they are raced too soon, too late, too much and too far. They must be mated to give their best performance. They are not given time to develop fully. They show signs of wear far too early, and at the right age they fall short of our expectations. This vicious circle repeats itself again and again. In the following season the young birds are once again thrown into the battle, since the old birds are not performing well.

Is it, perhaps, a question of the character of the breeder? After all, who finds it easy to decide to withdraw a good bird from racing before it is spent and keep it entirely for breeding? I know some fanciers, though, who resolutely withdraw one or more five-year olds every year and 'stock' them, even though they could still win very good prizes. Why not? They have plenty of younger athletes who fly even faster. In exchange, one pair of the 'retired' birds that has produced inferior offspring in

The fancier, his qualifications for success

the preceding season has to go. I have known even two-year olds find their way into the breeding loft because their offspring were better than they themselves.

It goes without saying that such radical measures, which are signs of sound judgement and common sense, enhance a breeder's reputation. The successful fancier is often called a 'knowledgeable' breeder. Few people realize that success is not so much a question of knowledge but of character.

A pigeon racing journalist is often asked for advice by unsuccessful fanciers, who consider him an expert. But who really knows a pigeon? There is much that is unknown, even to the most experienced fancier. We know little about the many factors which combine to make a pigeon a good flier. However, there are certain things that are apparent, obvious faults that represent a serious handicap, and if they appear in a pigeon then that pigeon must be got rid of.

Whenever I am asked for advice by a fancier I talk to him before giving it. He must know what my advice is based on. I might say to him, 'I will make the same decision as I would if they were my own pigeons. Even the good ones must go; only the best may remain. We always feed too many birds. Everybody races good pigeons these days, but only the best win. The best pigeon is the one that wins prizes regularly, some of them top prizes. It has earned its food. If it wins only top prizes, it is a crack.' In the end the fancier, who is, after all, master of his own loft, does what he likes. He does not need to follow my advice.

In most cases the fancier is an enthusiast. I have hardly ever visited a loft which could not have benefited from considerable weeding out. But I have never been certain when I left whether it really would be done. It usually transpired that all the pigeons remained just as they were. My selection would have been much too ruthless, at least in the eyes of that particular fancier.

It is difficult to make people understand that a young bird will never acquire anything it hasn't already got. It will not 'outgrow' any physical handicap nor will this disappear at

The fancier, his qualifications for success

moulting time. On the other hand, a pigeon can easily lose the virtues it has as a result of the fancier's mismanagement.

Frequently, a young bird that would not pass my selection test flies well or even very well. I then say to the fancier, 'All right, if you must keep it, race it to death, but do not use it for breeding.' This is usually the case with pigeons that have a defect which is not apparent in the parents. Such defects in the offspring very often indicate a general decline in the loft, with youngsters failing to come up to the standard of the older birds. The fancier does not see it, or does not want to see it. It is strange that these imperfect birds are often preferred to youngsters which perform less well but are in perfect physical shape. Such underrated young birds may show promise as yearlings and they should be given a chance.

The most common fault found in youngsters is absence of back. There's nothing there when you press on the junction of the tail with the back. The vent bones are too far removed from the breastbone. They give to the slightest pressure and their tips bend like rubber. If they are raced on the natural system and with a following wind, these early-bred youngsters may occasionally win good prizes. Nevertheless, they are not worth keeping and should be rejected, though it is not easy to convince a young breeder of this.

This brings me to my third point, the need for an *observant eye*. To observe something is not the same as to see it.

Let us assume, for example, that there is some peculiarity about the wing of a certain pigeon. The owner spreads out the wing and sees—nothing. He overlooks it, or perhaps he can see the singularity but attaches no importance to it. He is making a great mistake. Another fancier looks at the pigeon, spreads out the wing—and he *sees* it, although it is the same wing he is looking at. If he has never seen the unusual feature before, it arouses his interest. He wants to know how this will affect the pigeon, what results it might have. He considers the phenomenon with care and benefits from his observation. If he

The fancier, his qualifications for success

has seen it before, then he can immediately voice his judgement of the bird. A fancier like this one has an observant eye, the quality of a born breeder.

In my book, *You and I on Pigeons*, I wrote: 'I believe a breeder must be born as such. If he hasn't already got a special gift he will never acquire it. With patient tenacity, a keen eye and ear, he can acquire a certain skill. But success comes only with experience and long years of training.' I see no reason for altering a single word of this. The born breeder works very largely by intuition. He observes the truth instinctively, and can feel instinctively that something is important.

My father, who came from Lommel, in what was then (1863) the unspoilt moorland of Cempen, was a born fisherman and hunter, a real poacher, my mother used to say. He managed to make a catch where many another came home empty-handed. I remember we walked to Uitbergen one day. Suddenly my father stopped and said, 'A hare's been past here last night.' We children looked round but could see nothing. Father bent down and picked up some droppings. When he rubbed them between his thumb and forefinger, they were as dry as dust, so the hare must have been there quite some time ago. When we passed the same spot in the evening we had forgotten all about it, but my father said, 'He has just been here.' There were fresh droppings by the wayside. He counted the rows in the potato field and showed us exactly where he thought the hare must have his burrow. 'If I had a stick three foot long I could go and hit him behind the ears.' But there was no stick handy just then. A hare that any of us had tried to catch in this way would have shown us a clean pair of heels, but for a born hunter he would just sit there and wait to be caught. Later that week we did have hare for dinner, so there must have been a stick around the house somewhere.

Jef Van Riel told me once that he considered the late Gust De Feyter to have been the greatest expert on pigeons. I heard the following story about Gust in a café in Antwerp one day. A well-known breeder from the provinces had come to town to

The fancier, his qualifications for success

exhibit his pigeons. A number of young fanciers were standing by the cages when Gust joined them. After studying the birds carefully for some moments he said, 'Are those his best pigeons? If he doesn't think of something quick he'll have no loft in a few years' time.'

Everyone who heard him was shocked. Surely the man wouldn't say such a thing unless he knew what he was talking about? It turned out later that Gust had been right. What was it that Gust had noticed? What we all notice when it is too late, what the good, average breeder notices when the decline is just setting in, and what the real expert notices when there is as yet nothing to be seen. He feels instinctively that there is something in the wind; there is no other way of explaining it.

When Jef Van Riel paid Gust De Feyter this highest of compliments he added, 'In the end Gust got a bit past it. You can hardly believe that your judgement isn't so good any longer when you get older. It was the same with me. When I had to start wearing glasses I got worse.'

Jef is taciturn by nature. It is not easy to get him to talk, especially in the company of other fanciers. I still remember one time in Brasschaat when we were watching the international cycling race, the 'Brasschaat Eight', from Jef Roelens' ground-floor windows. The riders had to pass right in front of us. I cannot remember exactly who else was with us, but there were Rene Stijnen, Jan Marissen, Louis Pepermans. As the cyclists made their circuits we discussed the chances of Stanneken Ockers, German De Rycke, Rik I and the rest of them (for it was long ago). In between, we had a look at Roelens' pigeons, of course. We left no feather in his loft unturned. Everyone gave his opinion, but Jef Van Riel remained silent. When we pressed him to say something all we finally got out of him was, 'If all of you think that this pigeon or that is a good one then I suppose you must be right.' He liked to keep his thoughts to himself and brushed aside all arguments by saying, 'What do we *really* know of pigeons?'

Because he was so uncommunicative, I prepared my questions

The fancier, his qualifications for success

beforehand and tried to get them all in at convenient times during my visit. I am afraid I did not altogether succeed.

The problem of getting older and having to wear glasses had caught up with Jef unexpectedly. 'You see,' he said, 'at one time I used to be able to take in the scene at a glance as soon as I opened the loft door in the mornings. I knew exactly: this one is all right, this one is coming on, and that one will be a few more days. Now I have to pick them up one by one, and even then it isn't the same as it used to be.'

When I visited Jef Van Riel in Donk in June of that year it was my first visit since the previous September. He had driven into town when I arrived, so I had an opportunity to look at his pigeons. Some were sitting in the loft, others were left to fly around, for Jef no longer had the time nor the inclination to look after them.

When he returned home and had garaged his car I began, 'I've watched your birds flying. There are still some outstanding ones among them.' He only shrugged his shoulders, but I did not give up. I held up three fingers, and spread them out to indicate the three outer flight feathers, feathers with ventilation gaps between them wide enough to pass a pea through. Jef had to laugh. 'So you've noticed it, too,' he said. 'As the widower birds fly round and round the loft you can see some of them that don't flap their wings. They just drift along with the others, and they are just as fast. Those are the ones with the three feathers. Their wings don't move at all, only the outer flights do. They vibrate. Did you see that? they actually *vibrate!*'

I had already read about this phenomenon in scientific books. Professor Slijper and others have noticed and filmed it in large birds of prey which frequently spend hours circling in the air, moving their wings almost imperceptibly. Jef had noticed this in his pigeons and not just recently either. That is what is meant by being observant. Every fancier likes to watch his pigeons fly round the loft, but do we all see the right things? Seeing and observing are not necessarily the same.

When the famous 'De Donk' team entered fourteen birds in

The fancier, his qualifications for success

the Libourne race and all fourteen were placed among the leaders, Vermeijen said, 'Name the five top breeders and Jef will be among them. But he is the best of all the five at getting out of a pigeon all it has to give.'

I liked listening to Vermeijen. There was always something to to be learned from him. It is true, you have to be a born breeder to get the full potential out of a pigeon. You have to be able to see what there is to be seen, to sense what is in the making.

Take Louis Pepermans. He has a pigeon that he called *Little 021* (6419021-60). He put this cock into my hand after it had moulted in 1960 saying, 'He is going to be a good one.'

'How did he perform as a youngster?' I asked.

'Trained as far as Dourdan, nothing special, but he always came back,' he said.

'How is *Little 021* doing?' I asked him after the moult the following year.

'He went as far as Orleans. Five races, five tail-enders. But he is going to be good.'

The following year: 'Noyon, too late (and I still insist he's going to be good), St. Denis, too late (never mind, you'll see, he'll turn out one of my best birds).'

If a fancier speaks with such conviction it is best not to argue with him; not with Pepermans anyway, who will rarely be swayed once he has made up his mind.

In nine races *Little 021* never failed that year, he always came top of the list: from Orleans in the Malines and Zottegem clubs, from Dourdan in the Lier club, from Bourges and Orleans in the Merchtem club, duplicated into the Brabant Union. In this last race he finished first club, third Union, heavily pooled in both. He always won the pools and prizes. At Zemst, *Little 021* was the best of 39 widower cocks, after the blue 934. Whenever the bird was mentioned after that I always wanted to know on what Pepermans had based his prediction that he would be a top racer.

'Because he always had such good manners!'

He had selected 39 birds for the season. They all won top

The fancier, his qualifications for success

prizes, some of them several firsts. They did so well that there was no room for any other prizes on the commemorative plaque!

I have heard others say that 'good manners' promise a good bird. What exactly are good manners? It is not always easy to find words to explain something like this. When I queried further, I was told, 'It was as clear as daylight. A willing bird, always in fine shape; anyone could have picked him out of a crowd.' Anyone? That's saying too much. Perhaps another born breeder, a man with an eye for pigeons, could have picked him out.

Finally, I would like to quote an example of my own observation. I had gone to see a fancier and his son who were highly satisfied with their pigeons. One more race from Dourdan and they would have finished the season on the right side. There was one yearling, though, which had not come up to scratch. I was asked for my opinion.

'Has he won any prizes?' I asked.

'Yes, but nothing special.'

'Can't he do any better?'

Father and son looked at each other.

'He has been in the basket every Sunday from the end of April until now, the middle of July. We first raced him on the natural system, then on widowerhood. He's unreliable, gets a prize when there's no money at stake. He came eleventh once, but we hadn't put anything on him. The following week we put a fortune on him—he was a tail-ender. He did that to us twice. Shall we give him another season? Or shall we put him in the breeding loft?'

I said no to the last question, because I had noticed something about the bird. Twice while I had been there he had flown straight up from the loft floor to the skylight, like a lark.

I suggested racing the yearling from Dourdan (226 miles) and putting a full bet on him—at my expense. I wanted to bear the risk. After hesitating slightly, the fanciers accepted my proposal. But they were to nominate the rest of the birds.

I have kept the prize list. The second-nominated pigeon won

The fancier, his qualifications for success

4th prize, the yearling the 42nd. Together they won the first nominated series of two and the fourth unnominated one. They won 3,051 francs (about £25). Of course, I was running the risk that the bird would fail me, but the fact that he had won two top prizes proved that he could do it, and his behaviour made me 90 per cent sure that he was in peak form. Who would have hesitated to run such a risk? Either the two fanciers had never noticed the bird's behaviour, or they had attached no importance to it. What other explanation could there be? Whatever the reason, they were certainly unobservant. Later on, I told them what I had noticed about the bird's behaviour, and in fact they had not even seen it.

What should be said about *memory*?

Some people have a reputation for having a poor memory. They admit that they are forgetful. If you send them on an errand, they come back with too much, or too little, or even empty-handed. The next time you write the message down for them; they put the note in a safe place and promptly forget where they have put it.

We all know the popular remedy for a poor memory—tie a knot in your handkerchief. But what happens then if you forget to blow your nose? All this goes to show that some people have a good memory and others have a poor one. But we should beware of judging rashly. What do the experts have to say? Modern psychologists reject the notion that anyone is born with a defective memory. A small minority of people suffer from an organic abnormality of the brain which may eventually, around the age of 60 or 70, affect the memory to some degree. Illness, arteriosclerosis or excess of alcohol may speed up this process, but in 95 per cent of all cases the memory is quite intact.

There is the well-known story about the professor who lectured his table-companions on the inadvisability of eating fruit without peeling it because of the risk of infection. Since cherries cannot be peeled, he rinsed them in a glass of water. When he had eaten the last cherry, he promptly drank the water. A typical

The fancier, his qualifications for success

absent-minded professor. Absent-minded, yes, but not forgetful. Nor did he have a poor memory.

Here is a personal story. Once I had to collect an urgent prescription in town, with only ten minutes left before the shops closed. When I returned, my wife was standing in the door and she asked me what had kept me so long. And why had I not come back by car? By car? I turned on my heel to go and fetch the car—which was still standing in front of the chemist's.

How did it happen? I was just writing an article for *De Duif* and, as always, thinking about nothing else. Even on my way to the chemist and back I was mulling it over. I never make any written notes for my articles and reports but rely entirely on my memory. So this mishap, like the case of the absent-minded professor, was a question of concentration. My whole mind had been concentrated on one thing and everything else had been shut out.

This is why, at the beginning of this chapter, I mentioned ability to concentrate as one of the vital qualities a good fancier and breeder must possess. Anyone who wants to make a good job of something, who wants to create something of permanent importance, be it in his profession or hobby, must concentrate all his thoughts on his plan. He must be completely involved in it and allow nothing and no one to distract him.

In Belgium, we are too easily satisfied when it comes to organizing something. We do not go to a great deal of trouble but hope that in the end everything will sort itself out. The majority of our fanciers are guilty of this kind of negligence. But a top-class breeder plans everything in advance, down to the smallest detail. This is why the best breeders refer to themselves as the slaves of their pigeons, and in many cases they are quite correct.

Probably it is not necessary to go to quite such lengths; a little less would suffice. But I know some people, very successful in their work, who leave nothing to chance. They concentrate completely on their business or profession. Yet when it comes to their pigeons, they go to the other extreme and leave everything to chance.

The fancier, his qualifications for success

One sure way to develop your memory, which is a real help in concentrating on your pigeons, is to make written notes of everything that happens. I know of no one who does this more thoroughly than Octaaf De Jonghe from Wezembeek-Oppem; he can answer any question about every single pigeon he has raced or bred, right back to the date he took up the sport. He keeps a card file. I would not go so far as to say that keeping a card file is absolutely essential to success in pigeon racing, but is it asking too much to make a note of which pairs have been mated each year? To note the ring numbers of the youngsters? To keep a record of every youngster, what happened to it, whether it was healthy or ill, whether, where and why it was lost, whether it was trained or raced as a youngster, a yearling or an adult pigeon? Is it too much to keep notes on races, on wind and weather, temperature and distance, number of birds entered, finishing position, and total number of entries in each race? It takes little more than a quarter of an hour per week to keep such a record.

As you keep your file, your notes will gradually expand because you will learn to draw conclusions from your observations. You will see the connection between certain facts and develop a better eye for pigeons in general and your own in particular. With the help of such reliable notes you will be able to breed and race with much less risk.

I now come to the fifth and last item in my list: *planning*.

The fancier who has patience and strength of character, who pursues his sport by observation and concentration, will automatically draw up a detailed programme. Everything is planned in advance; nothing is left to chance. He knows which birds will be racing next season, which have to be kept and which will have to go. After the moult he selects his youngsters and yearling. He knows from experience which points will guide his choice, which requirements the birds must meet. The mating dates of the breeding pairs and the widower birds are fixed. He knows whether he will breed youngsters from his racers, how many, or whether he will take the eggs away. He also knows why.

The fancier, his qualifications for success

He draws on experience and he has learned from his mistakes. After all, he is not blind. He has drawn up a racing programme for his pigeons. But if this has to be altered unexpectedly he is never unprepared. As far as he is concerned there are no insoluble problems. He has given it all careful thought.

Patience, character, observation, concentration and planning —these five go hand in hand. Where they are applied everything will go smoothly.

When breeders meet they discuss every imaginable aspect of pigeon racing. They scrutinize the birds (you must have the best!), stress the importance of the loft, the method of feeding. All too often feeding is not given the attention it deserves. Then there is the breeding system, the method of training and racing. Are they not equally important? And so they go on and on, discussing which is the more important: the bow, the string or the arrow.

For many years now I have been in close contact with fanciers, their pigeons and their theories, and I have kept my eyes and ears open. My main interest has always been in the fancier himself, the man behind the sport. What then is my final conclusion? I can sum it up in a remark Jef Van Riel once made: 'In my opinion the breeder counts for 80 per cent. Give him a loft of duds, and six months later he will have put it to rights. One year later he will be racing. Watch him!'

You may be inclined to dismiss this as empty talk. But it is a truth that applies to the rich and the poor, the academically minded and the working man. It goes for every kind of fancier. For this reason I have gone to some length in this chapter in considering the human element in our sport. I hope you will benefit from it.

So much for the qualifications of the fancier. Now we must consider the fancier's dependence on other people, for without them we could not have our sport. Who does the fancier depend on?

The officers of his club, and, to a great extent, the liberators, the transporters, truck-drivers, train-drivers—even a friend who

The fancier, his qualifications for success

volunteers to carry his birds on a training toss, and the friend he entrusts with the management of his loft when he goes on holiday. These are only a few.

When we decide to become fanciers, we usually join a club, so that we can compete with the other members. We had nothing to do with the selection of the officers, or the club's policies or activities. Until we become used to the club's activities we are practically outsiders, and even when we are completely orientated we have only one vote to elect officers or change policies. As newcomers we must be wary of proposing changes (even for the better) or we will soon find ourselves the most unpopular member. Organizations hate to have their accustomed routine changed, even when the change brings distinct advantage. So as club members *we are dependent*!

Every fancier has to put himself at the mercy of the man who transports his birds. Will they bring the pigeons home if the weather does not warrant a release? Are their station wagons or vans roomy enough? Is the ventilation good? On hot days, is there a fan to move the air? I know of two large crates of homers which were put under the roof of an uninsulated truck and when the crates were opened the birds staggered out and fell to the ground. The owners of the birds in those crates had put their faith in the wrong person.

In my columns in *De Duif*, I have made frequent reference to the studies in Germany, England, the U.S.A., on the subject of navigation-homing. How do the pigeons find their way home? Once it was believed that a pigeon was drawn to its loft as a nail is drawn to a magnet; the pigeon could pinpoint its home and fly unerringly towards it. Today we know that this is nonsense. Volumes have been written on the subject of homing but how many liberators, either the man at home or the man at the liberation point, have ever read a word of this valuable information? No, liberations are made week after week, and thousands of pigeons are lost just as often, because the men on whom fanciers depend are ignorant of scientific findings.

In Belgium, we have a saying that if you don't have pigeons to

The fancier, his qualifications for success

cull at the end of a season you cannot improve your stock. I have a letter from an American correspondent in which he says that he expects to start his young bird team with sixty to seventy youngsters each year and end up with seven or eight. This has gone on year after year. I wrote to him that if his practise was correct, his seven or eight surviving birds should by now be absolutely invincible. The fact that the man's racing results had not improved should have shown him long ago that he was indeed wasting pigeons.

The man who tells you that you should be glad to be rid of those pigeons you lose in a smash race is an ignorant one. We often find that pigeons we value most, or those we bet most heavily on, are the ones most likely to go astray in a rain smash. They will fight harder than birds with less courage. When less courageous birds find a safe shelter from a storm, the best keep trying until they are washed out and often lost.

This does not apply to birds lost in a head-wind too severe to fly against. The stronger the wind, the lower the flight of the birds, and many are killed by obstacles like wires, aerials, or even wire netting stretched across a field.

Every liberator should be a man who has shown that he has sound judgement, and that he is a man who can be depended on. He must not be an instinctive gambler, because a gambler is inclined to take foolish risks. He should be a man who has demonstrated that he can handle money. Every bird raced is surely worth four or five British pounds or ten American dollars. In a 1,000 bird race, there is at least £5,000 on the field. Who would dream of putting so much money into the hands of a man who had never demonstrated that he could handle it? Yet pigeon clubs frequently do just that. Not only do they permit men with poor judgement to liberate but such men have never demonstrated that they can handle any goods of great value. The Chinese have a saying, 'Fool me once, shame on *you*: fool me twice shame on *me*.' When members of a pigeon club let a man who has shown bad judgement liberate a second time and they lose precious birds, then it is the members of the club

The fancier, his qualifications for success

who should be ashamed of having allowed the same liberator to take charge again.

Some day I hope to see, in every country, examinations that determine the qualifications of liberators. There are students of homing and atmospheric conditions who could compose the questions for such examinations. There is an abundance of reading material to be studied by every prospective liberator. If he is too lazy to read it or too stupid to understand it, he should certainly not be chosen for such an important job. No one would want to depend on such a man.

We are dependent on many others, from the feed merchants whom we expect to deliver grain that is clean and without mould or mildew, to the drug manufacturers and the researchers who are diligently examining the causes of pigeon diseases (paratyphoid, for example) to find the drugs or vitamins which will effect cures. In some countries we are even dependent on the goodwill of our neighbours when local authorities seek to outlaw pigeons.

2

The selection of breeding stock

The qualities of the true fancier reveal themselves from the moment he takes up the sport. He focusses his entire attention on breeding. Racing is of secondary importance and only serves as a test that shows the breeder whether he has chosen the right way or whether he has to start afresh. Breeding must always be of paramount importance throughout a fancier's career, for it is the key to success.

In pairing a cock and a hen we bring together two birds of the same species that have a certain similarity. I say 'certain', because there *are* differences, however few. The offspring of this pair differ both from their parents and each other. If we are breeding from first-class stock we expect the progeny to match their parents, if not surpass them, in flying ability, physique and general racing qualities. This, then, is our aim: to produce top stock and top fliers.

A few days after mating there are two eggs in the nest bowl. Do you know exactly how an egg comes into being? I have always looked on it as a small miracle, but it was years before I found out how it is produced. How many fanciers can explain the origin and development of this miracle or know what happens up to the moment when the egg is laid?

How long does it take until a young pigeon is mature? It depends on the time it is hatched. If a bird is hatched early in January it can be expected to reach sexual maturity in four or five months, though differences are also caused by environ-

The selection of breeding stock

mental factors. If the youngsters are segregated they mature later than if they are kept together with adult birds. Food, loft conditions (temperature, light) and other factors also have some influence. Quite apart from this, some strains mature earlier than others. It is generally true to say that long-distance birds take longer to reach maturity than short-distance birds. The latter also take a shorter time to become fully-grown.

Under the influence of hormones released into the bloodstream by the glands as soon as the hen comes into contact with another bird of her species (it need not necessarily be of the opposite sex) the eggs begin to be formed in the ovary. In their book *Le Pigeon Voyageur* (a standard work which should not be absent from the library of any fancier who wishes to compare his experience with scientific findings) Dr. Lahaye and Dr. Cordiez, both professors at the veterinary college at Kuregem (Brussels), give a description of the remarkable evolution of the egg-cell clearing its way from the ovary to the nest bowl. It's really fascinating. Anyone wanting to know more should buy the book which will provide him with a great deal of other highly interesting information.

After the hatching period a small, helpless ball of fluff emerges from the egg, with a disproportionately large beak and two ugly dark spots, the eyes, waiting to open up and admit daylight.

How many fanciers know that they can assist in the creation of this 'miracle' called an egg? The separation of the mature egg from the ovaries is so critical that it only happens in the evening, about 8 o'clock, when the hen is quite undisturbed. The bird will be standing motionless in its nest at that moment and should be left entirely alone. Nor should it be disturbed during the following two days and especially at the moment when the egg, usually with a great effort, is laid in the nest bowl.

What can we say about the fancier who races the hen and gambles with the exact time when the first egg will be laid? He expects the hen to make a greater effort than usual to reach her nest. This *may* happen, but it is just as likely that the opposite will occur. I personally would not rely too much on this system.

The selection of breeding stock

There are too many cases where the hen comes down to the nearest available loft to get rid of her egg in a hurry. If this happens there is always the risk that she will adopt her new home and be lost to her owner.

There are a lot of old wives' tales about pigeons' eggs. One maintains that the first egg is always a hen, the second a cock, or vice versa. But what about the many cases when two hens or two cocks are hatched together? Does an egg show any signs of what kind of pigeon will come from it? One fancier will say yes, the other no, and the third will think it a ridiculous question.

Everyone is entitled to his opinion. But if you are ever invited to choose an egg, take one which is well-shaped and has a distinctly different shape at either end, with one end rounded and the other more or less pointed. Never take a completely round egg. Select one with a smooth shell, preferably matt white in colour, without darker lines in it. Always take the largest. If you follow these rules you stand a good chance of getting a healthy baby pigeon.

Apart from the signs visible on the outside of the egg, there are certain other points that must guide our choice. If possible, choose an egg from the pair that laid first, and, as a second choice, from the pair with the shortest interval between the first two layings. Finally, take the egg which is 'cleanest'. These are three features indicating health and vitality. They promise vigorous pigeons, which is what you want.

Then you have to wait and see what emerges from this fragile shell in which a sperm and an ovum—both microscopically small—have started a new life. The combination of chromosomes and genes will decide whether the hatched bird is a dud or a crack. Let no one try to tell me that the result can be foreseen; that two pigeons of the best stock were mated together and consequently . . . Nothing of the kind!

The term 'blood relation' is still in common use. Its use is quite unjustified, for modern biology has established that the hereditary factors of parents are not passed on to their children through the blood but solely through the genes of the chromo-

The selection of breeding stock

somes. Before the Austrian monk and scientist Gregor Mendel made his significant contribution to modern genetics, the 'blood theory' was predominant. Even the great Charles Darwin, founder of the idea of 'natural selection of breeding', subscribed to it.

Galton and other biologists after him conducted experiments in which blood transfusions and ovary transplants in black and white varieties of rabbits and chickens were to prove the theory of 'blood relationship'. But the experiments failed entirely, for the progeny of the animals thus treated did not turn out mottled in colour. (*Evolution, Genetics and Man* by Professor Th. Dobzhansky.) It is not blood, but the chromosomes in the sperms and ova which are the carriers of the genes, the hereditary factors.

I have no intention of going into elaborate scientific explanations, because they would be of little use to pigeon fanciers. But I feel bound to explain a few basic scientific theories in order to show that 'mating and breeding' is a tricky game. We can then decide which rules must be observed to obtain the best results with the means available.

What are chromosomes? They are tiny, thread-like bodies contained in the nucleus of a cell. Each species has its own number of chromosomes. The sperm of a pigeon cock, for example, contains thirty-one. They differ in shape and size, but each individual chromosome is always constant in shape and size in any particular species. When the nucleus of the sperm, which has half the regular number, unites with that of the ovum, which also has half, each chromosome takes up a position alongside the corresponding chromosome of the other cell, thus forming pairs.

What are genes? They are bodies of molecular dimensions. The number of genes contained in every sex cell is unknown. So far we do not know the number for a single organism, but scientists believe it runs into several thousands. In man, it is thought to be between 10,000 and 100,000. Each gene may control certain characteristics, but most characteristics are determined by more than one gene. As the sperm of a pigeon

The selection of breeding stock

cock unites with the ovum of a hen, the number of chromosomes is doubled. Nobody can predict what developes from this fertilized egg, because every new life is a new combination of thousands of hereditary factors contributed by the parents, grandparents, great grandparents, etc. The egg reflects its forebears. We must wait and see how we have cast the dice. If many favourable hereditary factors combine in the new life, we have cast well. But if its ancestors had a large number of characteristics undesirable in our sport, we would have been better advised not to gamble at all. We will once more get the same number of chromosomes typical of the species but with an entirely new combination of genes.

All this shows clearly that in selecting our breeding stock we must find those elements which give us the best chances of success.

The things I look for when selecting birds for breeding are: *good health*, *vitality* and *pedigree*.

Why do I frequently use the words 'thoroughly healthy' in my weekly articles? Would not 'healthy' by itself be enough? My aim is to emphasize again and again that you can never give too much attention to the perfect health of all the pigeons in your loft. Thoroughly healthy means healthy to the core, one hundred per cent healthy, call it what you may.

I am completely convinced that a large number of our pigeons are not healthy. I do not mean that they are ill, but it is certain that many miss winning prizes or come in at the tail end of a race because something is wrong with their health. Being healthy and not being ill are two different things. All the time, pigeons which are actually ill are being put into baskets without their owners being aware of this. Strictly speaking, before every race a vet ought to inspect every single pigeon before it is basketed. There would be astonished faces all round, as many pigeons would be refused a clean bill of health. Why? Because of the danger of infection to other healthy birds.

I remember the following incident. I was visiting a loft which contained a three-year old cock that had been an outstanding

The selection of breeding stock

flier as a youngster and yearling. No one could say that the breeder had over-taxed the bird. He followed a system by which he raced his youngsters no further than Noyon (140 miles) and his yearlings no further than St. Denis (196 miles) or Dourdan (226 miles). Only the two-year olds were basketed for every race as far as Angoulême (463 miles). He raced on widowerhood, from the last Sunday in April to the first Sunday in August. A classical system, in my opinion, and a breeder who acted with deliberation.

Well, the bird looked healthy enough, but as a two-year old it had only won tail-end prizes. What was wrong with it? Had it had a bad moult? Was it lack of muscle tone? Was there anything to be seen in its throat? The loft was healthy, the food good, the nest boxes clean. There was no sign of anything being amiss. The whole thing seemed a puzzle.

I asked whether he had bred from the bird. Why did I ask this question? Because you know the tree by its fruit. I consider this approach logical. If I can detect nothing in the adult that will give me a clue, I turn to the youngsters. As a two-year old, the bird had bred a squab which had died in the nest shortly after it had been ringed. Perhaps the hen was to blame. The following year the cock was given a new mate. One egg was unfertilized. The squab hatched from the second egg made very poor progress. I felt the youngster's crop and throat and noticed a small lump which prevented food from passing along the gullet. It was obviously canker. It is not difficult to dislodge such a growth from the gullet and by massage get it into the throat from where it can be removed. In any case, the youngster had to be got rid of.

I have every reason to believe that the cock had never been really healthy. In a personal letter to me Dr. Whitney, our American veterinarian and friend, says, 'Canker, another protozoa disease, is easily held in check with Amino-nithro-thiozole. *All* pigeons are carriers. In post mortems on 7,000 birds all over the world all were found to harbour the organisms in their crops.' In *Keep Your Pigeons Flying* Dr. Whitney writes,

The selection of breeding stock

'In general these are harmless organisms found in the crops of most, if not all, pigeons. They apparently lie in wait for some constitutional weakening in the pigeon's body to produce the disease we call canker.'

I would like to emphasize this again: 'harmless', 'lie in wait for some constitutional weakness'. As far as the three-year old cock was concerned, I came to the conclusion that he was no longer thoroughly healthy (or never had been). Was this a case of weakening? If so, what was the cause? I do not know.

How do we weaken our pigeons?

We start them too soon and stop racing and breeding too late. We do not allow them enough rest after a hard race or basket them without a break Sunday after Sunday. After a difficult or unsuccessful race, we do not look after them as we should. Or perhaps their food is insufficient, unsuitable or unwholesome. The loft may be at fault, too, by failing to meet the most elementary requirements: too damp, too cold, excessive and sudden fluctuations in temperature, draught, not enough sun, lack of fresh air, overcrowding.

On the other hand, it is conceivable that we were not observant enough when we bought a strange bird. It may have been doped, a practice which always results in decline afterwards. Perhaps the new pigeon brought parasites or diseases with it. I will come back to some of these points later on.

Correct treatment can cure a pigeon of trichonomas. It is then worth keeping it for breeding, but in most cases I would say it was spoiled for racing.

Many pigeons that have been cured of coccidiosis are henceforth immune to the disease, but they remain carriers and infect other birds in the loft. They do not pass on the disease to all birds but to those which are weakened and lack the necessary resistance because they are not one hundred per cent healthy.

Squabs are often found to have a yellow, cheesy deposit inside their beaks. These small yellow lumps always point to trichomoniasis. Experience teaches us to separate these youngsters from the other birds but ignore the symptoms otherwise, and in

The selection of breeding stock

a few days the lumps will have disappeared without any help from the fancier. The pigeon will grow up normally; it may turn into a crack racer and even produce good youngsters. I have experienced this myself.

The question remains: was the pigeon completely healthy? Which of the parents was to blame? Both of them? The youngster was not bound to go down with canker. Was it only threatened by the disease? I do not know. One thing is certain: its physical constitution got the better of the attack.

We must constantly be on our guard. The incident must not be repeated. If it is, the pigeon and all its offspring must be destroyed without mercy.

We study our pigeons for years and work out plans for building up a healthy strain that offers a reasonable chance of success in this sport, and then, in spite of all our efforts, despite all the time and money spent, our work is destroyed in a single stroke. We have made a mistake; we have been too soft; we have not been realistic.

The sole basis of success in our sport is the perfect health of our pigeons. They must be completely and wholly healthy in every respect and have a resilience that is indestructible. One thing is certain, if a seriously diseased pigeon is basketed together with others, half of them will be unable to resist infection unless previous disease has made them immune.

The outbreak of the disease may not always be immediate, but in most cases there will be certain signs which should arouse suspicion. Always watch the droppings of your birds. It is here that the first signs of danger can be recognized. As you clean out the loft each morning inspect the perch of each bird and the area round the nest bowls of the squabs.

If you have an outstanding pigeon, a crack, you know that it is in perfect health. There can be no doubt of that. If some of your pigeons do not come up to expectations, compare their droppings with those of your crack. If their food is the same and you can find no difference, their lack of performance shows simply that they are not in good health, or at least not as good

The selection of breeding stock

as your crack bird. If you do find a difference then something is amiss. The birds are not healthy, perhaps they are even diseased. It will pay you to investigate, not superficially, but thoroughly, if necessary with the help of a vet. Then you will have to take the consequences as far as your racing and breeding programme is concerned, and no half measures!

If one and the same loft houses pigeons which perform well and others which, in spite of the same environment and treatment, do not come up to scratch, and you are certain there are no intestinal parasites, there is only one remedy—get rid of them; they are not good. 'Cull them', I always say. But every factor must be given careful consideration. Let experience decide. There is only one alternative, cull them or have them on crutches for evermore. You are not likely to get good racing or breeding results from a pigeon which has been cured of an infectious disease.

After all this I can only say, judge for yourself in deciding which birds to select for breeding. The best is only just good enough, especially where health is concerned.

The word 'vitality' derives from the Latin *vita*, meaning 'life'. But vitality must not be confused with liveliness. The two words have quite different meanings. A vital pigeon may be lively, though; one does not exclude the other. But a restless pigeon, which we sometimes call *Zotteken* (mad, or foolish) since it will even chase its own shadow, because it is as nervous as the day is long, runs a risk of dropping out of the race prematurely because it is spent. Such pigeons are apt to age quickly because they mature quickly. They are hardly ever found in the medium or long-distance class.

The majority of pigeons which possess vitality have a calm, composed disposition. Vitality means the power to sustain life, to grow old and yet remain young. In other words, the physical functions remain active for a long time. Detrimental outside factors, environmental influences, everything a racing pigeon encounters, have no ill effect on such birds. This vitality is passed on to their offspring.

One of my friends had six outstanding breeding cocks and was

The selection of breeding stock

looking for a few top-class hens. He managed to purchase a yearling hen from Pepermans and he asked me to choose a suitable mate for her. The oldest of the cocks was from 1951, the youngest was a three-year old. I chose the oldest. He had been a crack flier. His youngsters made splendid progress. By comparison with other cocks he showed the least signs of wear. He showed vitality. For all these reasons I could justify my choice. But the final decision was up to the breeder; after all, he was the owner.

A week later I was asked to classify and reduce a loft. It was over-crowded and everything that was not up to scratch had to go. Of two youngsters bred by the same mother the elder was allowed to stay, the younger had to go. We passed along to the adult birds where I found a 1959 cock mated to a 1951 hen. The cock, from a second-rate loft, was no good. He had aged before his time. The hen came from the loft of the late Collard, a well-known fancier from Louvain. Her first mate, who had sired the youngster I had spared, was a 1956 cock, a fine Huyskens-Van Riel bought from Van Elsacker at Loenhout. These two were mated again and made an excellent breeding pair, which was to be expected considering their pedigree. The 1959 cock was culled.

Many fanciers are not easily convinced. Frequently, they can see nothing in the appearance of the feathering, the feel of the muscles. Sometimes a bird can be judged by the appearance of its eyes; whether they are clear and sparkling or dull and lifeless can be evidence of the superiority of an older bird over a much younger one.

Another thing to which I always draw a fancier's attention is the seventh flight feather. In old pigeons which are still unweakened by age, this feather remains smooth, shiny and straight-quilled. I will come back to the seventh feather later. In pigeons which mature and age prematurely, the flights become hard, dry and deformed quite early in life. Their muscles waste, their eyes become dull, their racing performance deteriorates and the young they produce are of inferior quality.

The selection of breeding stock

Many fanciers are too slow to notice when a pigeon shows signs of declining, of ageing when others are still in their prime. Such a bird should not be used for breeding, because it lacks vitality.

The best age for stock pigeons is often discussed. Many breeders are against breeding from old birds. But why? Both old and young birds can produce equally good offspring. In the breeding loft of many a top-class fancier we may find birds of either sex who are great-great-grandparents. Birds of ten, twelve years or more are quite common. Loius Pepermans' *Goede Witzwing* (Good Whitewing), the ancestor of countless superb racers and producers, was hatched in 1947. It was not until 1962 that he showed the first signs of slight decline.

And what about Jef Van Riel's *Bange* (The Timid One), and all the other outstanding racers who were stocked after having flown many brilliant prize-winning races? For years they attracted to Ekeren-Donk many a fancier who wanted to acquire one or other of their descendants.

A fancier who races well but does not yet possess a number of old stock pigeons is still in the initial stages of pigeon racing. He has made a good start; the future looks promising. But the promise, the promise of vitality, has yet to be redeemed.

As a rule, the age of a breeding pigeon is nothing to go by, but it can be said that cocks usually last longer than hens. I personally breed from a cock as long as there is life in him. While I am, in principle, against giving pigeons vitamins, I do not hesitate to help an old cock with vitamin E, the fertility vitamin. This practice is common among experienced breeders and often shows good results.

With a hen things are slightly different. As long as old cocks and hens can produce sperms and egg cells respectively, these are of the same quality that they were years before when they were produced for the very first time. The chromosomes do not undergo any decline or deterioration. This is a scientific fact. Nevertheless, when an old hen is suspected of approaching physical decline, the youngsters bred from her must be watched

The selection of breeding stock

closely. If they show any signs of weakness whatsoever the wise fancier will intervene immediately. Why?

The hen produces the yolk and the albumen contained in the egg, the food for the growing embryo. A worn-out organism cannot be expected to yield high-quality food. A hen, therefore, has had her day sooner than a cock. To determine how long to use a cock, it is advisable to examine his throat. The throat of an old cock often shows a grey deposit, which means that the regurgitated food will be of inferior quality. This bird is too old, not too old to produce youngsters, but too old to feed them. But the feeding could be done by other birds.

The thing to do, then, is to breed from old birds as long as they produce sperms and lay nutritiously sound eggs, irrespective of their physical condition. But it is wise to let foster parents take care of the young once they are hatched. This is what Louis Vermeijen advised, and he was not one to commit his experiences to paper lightly.

At the same time this policy must not lead us to making another mistake. Our breeding loft must not become an Old Pigeons' Home. We should not hesitate, therefore, to stock a bird which is a good racer and producer and is full of vitality before it is too old. Too many first-class pigeons are sacrificed on the 'field of honour' and we regret not having stocked them in time. But then it is too late for remorse. We can boost the virility of a cock with vitamin E to a certain extent; but we should be careful not to overtax the strength of our pigeons thoughtlessly. We often ask too much of them, both in racing and breeding. Valuable pigeons deserve to be treated with consideration. The better we treat them the longer they will be of use to us. But this really belongs to another chapter.

When we see a pigeon advertised for sale, apart from noting its name and ring number (assuming that we know the breeder and his reputation) we will want to find out quite a bit of additional information, about the bird's line of descent, its *pedigree*. Why? Because we want to know what we are buying, what the pigeon is worth in terms of heredity. For this reason we want to

The selection of breeding stock

know what record as racers and breeders its parents and grandparents have had.

The long line of successes of pigeons is recorded in the *stud book*. It is the successes of a pigeon that determine the value of its offspring. During a discussion among fanciers someone once said, 'What do we really mean by "value"? Is it the intrinsic value or the market value? After all, clever advertising is seldom without effect.' This point could be discussed at length without fanciers ever entirely agreeing on it.

Both the market value and the intrinsic value of a pigeon depend on the reputation of the loft. Clever advertising can increase the market value. But this is an artificial, an inflated value. The fancier with sound judgment will ignore sales talk and concentrate on the facts. He will check and compare the data given for each pigeon offered for sale before he makes his choice.

The market value of a pigeon, unlike its intrinsic value, rises and falls according to supply and demand, as does the price of any commodity. Anything in short supply is expensive and a glut in any commodity sells it cheaply. For example, I believe that late-bred youngsters will fetch higher prices any year when there are heavy losses among both adult pigeons and youngsters. If a fancier has suffered heavy losses during a season he will naturally show more interest in the market than someone who has lost no birds, or only a few.

I will try to give a few words of advice to the fancier who contemplates a new acquisition. If all breeders were conscientious in keeping pedigrees of their pigeons, the choice would not be so difficult. The value of such a record is quite obvious.

I would like to bring up here the question of 'mating at a distance', by using the pedigree as the sole basis. More than once I have written about this in *De Duif*. As was to be expected, my views led to digs and jokes by my friends. But how could I show them? For some time I had promised to visit a friend and reader to advise him on breeding, but something had always prevented me from keeping my promise. He lived quite a distance away,

The selection of breeding stock

and he did not believe in free pairing; even Vermeijen's arguments left him unconvinced.

This friend had a record of each pigeon, giving the usual data on number of races flown, distances, number of pigeons entered, direction of wind, speeds of first and last pigeon home, daily temperature and prize gained. I asked him to send me these data and in addition list the parents and grandparents of all breeding birds and widower cocks that had produced youngsters. All in all, it was an incomplete pedigree of a limited number of pigeons belonging to a small breeder.

No man is a prophet in his own country, but I simply could not keep it to myself. I wrote an article on this method of pairing in *De Duif*, which, as I have already mentioned, my friends found very interesting.

At any event, my friend and I went ahead with our way of pairing, and we have done the same thing each year ever since. He now sends me his own suggestions together with the pedigree. I have never changed them, not would I have dared to. Only those pigeons which had produced good offspring were kept. Those which had not were destroyed. Youngsters and yearlings were judged by the basket. Good fliers whose speed had deteriorated over the years were given a trial in the breeding loft.

Was this a logical, a rational method of selection? Can we turn out a pigeon that has earned its keep, without reference to its build, its wings, its muscles? I say 'without reference', for I never saw the birds and had to judge from their racing and breeding records, and those of their parents. Was there any need to handle the birds, to select by appearance? Dr. Whitney was the only one who did not laugh when I told him about it and asked for his opinion. He told me another story.

In the United States a group of biologists were offered a large grant for undertaking scientific research into the factors that account for speed in race horses. My friend, Dr. Whitney, who is an expert on genetics, worked on the project. The aim was to find a scientific method of breeding the fastest possible

The selection of breeding stock

horses. The scientists were given every possible help and support, anything they needed in the way of equipment. They measured and weighed the fastest horses, they took all the data one can possibly take of a horse: its height, width, length, muscles, legs, loins and so on. Later all these data were evaluated; nothing was found, not a single clue that could have been considered a typical sign of speed. They were as wise as they had been at the outset. Had there been any pigeon fanciers among them they might possibly have found something, perhaps in the horses' eyes. But scientists are sober people, thank goodness!

All thoroughbred horses are built the same way; they stand high on slender legs and have a hollow abdomen, i.e. no 'belly'. When you see a race horse you always see the same type, and yet there is a difference . . . to those who know. And then at last they found the clue. The Jockey Club possessed the secret—the pedigree, the stud book.

In the stud book they found the ancestry of the fastest horses, which had produced the fastest foals, stallions, mares. It was here that they found the horses which possessed the 'speed' factor to the highest degree and had passed it on to their offspring, this factor which could not be determined by weights and measurements.

By its fruit so is the tree judged. The pedigree shows which animals possess the best combination of hereditary factors and promise the best combination of these factors in their offspring. The scientists found in the pedigree what they had failed to find eleswhere, the hereditary factors that control the athletic qualities in a horse, above all speed.

Which would you prefer? To pair pigeons by appearance, but without reliable data? Or at a distance with the help of a pedigree? In pairing and breeding you should take into consideration all the facts that appear useful to you, but always with an eye on the pedigree. If ever you are at your wits' end and cannot make up your mind, stop pondering and let the pedigree decide, nothing else.

Once again I would like to quote Dr. Whitney. In one of his

The selection of breeding stock

many letters he says, 'In Norway they have a proverb over 2,500 years old—If you would have good children, marry not the maid who is the only good maid in the clan. . . .' Translated into pigeon fanciers' language this means—if you want a good pigeon, get it from a loft that is known to have a large proportion of good birds. I hope I have made the point clear.

If you have the chance of acquiring a bird from a good loft, a loft that has a good reputation, then you should prefer this to a bird from a loft that has won a top prize 'as if by a miracle'. You might think that this is obvious. But how many fanciers are there who have no confidence in their own strain (because they lack patience or simply aren't good breeders and never will be) but who are always ready to buy new stock from other fanciers who have happened to score a few successes, however few or however long ago? For the sake of a few inferior birds and a chance success, they betray their own good birds, i.e. birds of a certain mean value.

Let me quote Dr.Whitney yet again, 'Suppose we take two pigeons as examples. They are equally good racers. One is the poorest of a remarkable family of racers, the other the best of a poor family. Which would you expect to produce the better offspring?' I repeat—both are equally good racers! If you are smart, you will choose the pigeon that is the worst of an outstanding loft.

We must not expect miracles from the youngsters produced by champion fliers. Crack birds will seldom produce cracks to match their parents. There is a limit to top performance which cannot be surpassed. But cracks can always be expected to produce just a few champions among a large number of average fliers. This will tempt the less experienced breeders to want to breed a large number of birds which outclass their parents. It has been scientifically established, however, that the value of a strain, a race or a species lies in the average, i.e. midway between the lowest point and the top.

Dr. Whitney, fancier and naturalist with years of experience, takes his advice a little further, 'If you want to choose good

The selection of breeding stock

breeding stock and you can afford to pay only so much,' (as is the case with 90 per cent of our fanciers) 'then buy a good bird from a top family in preference to an even better bird from a poor performing family.'

A writer on racing pigeons has to be familiar with Mendel's teachings and know something of biology and biochemistry, even if it is only the basic principles. But breeding pigeons is not the same as growing peas and maize. In breeding pigeons we constantly look for something better, for perfection. In a way it is the same with growing maize, and yet there is a difference. You can grow maize on many acres of land. You get a crop every year from which you can eliminate those elements which are considered detrimental or undesirable, and these elements are known. In the case of pigeons only a few are known. For most of the time we are fumbling in the dark.

With pigeons, all the important elements can be expressed in two words—racing ability. Fanciers who have read my first booklet (*You and I on Pigeons*) published in 1948, and those who read *De Duif* regularly, know what Dr. Bom thought about it, 'Racing ability is made up of many factors, most of which we do not know. Nor do we know how these factors are related to one another.'

There is no direct method in dealing with pigeons. They can only be judged by their flying performance. Years can be spent on it. Once you have managed to breed certain features into your pigeons and got rid of others you can never know whether some good hereditary factors were lost along with some of the bad ones, or whether some undesirable factors crept into you new strain alongside the good ones. The basket will have to be the judge.

This is why, in my opinion, Mendelian methods can scarcely be applied to pigeon breeding. Experience, patience, an observant eye and intuition are more important when it comes to selection. Imagine talking to a group of renowned breeders at a championship and asking them, 'May we ask you when you first applied Mendel's theory to your loft? Surely you wouldn't be giving away a secret by telling us?' I am convinced that none of them would take the question seriously.

The selection of breeding stock

In my whole career as a breeder and writer I have only heard one breeder talk of Mendel and his theory, and he only did so because I insisted. It was Louis Vermeijen, and we were talking about the breeding of types. Afterwards he said to me, 'Don't mention this to any serious breeder. Any serious breeder would rather let the basket decide when selecting, or rely on the pedigree when buying new stock.' The pedigree is an indispensible criterion in selecting birds for mating and in finding a new, true-bred strain for cross-breeding.

To sum it up, I would like to say that to me health, vitality and pedigree are the most important factors governing my choice of breeding stock. And once again I must stress that health is not the same as vitality. A pigeon that has vitality is always healthy. It is well known that a champion is never ill. He dies of old-age. But a healthy pigeon does not necessarily have vitality. Some healthy pigeons show signs of wear very early in life. They are useless for building up a strain and keeping it at a certain standard. The difference between the two lies in their 'durability'.

We often hear of this or that fancier having been on the lookout for good birds. But he will not breed from them unless they have passed their test in the basket. Anything he buys must first of all prove its racing ability.

On the other hand, I have never introduced foreign 'blood' into my loft, except for breeding purposes alone.

Put the emphasis on breeding, and you will do well in racing.

Many will ask: 'But why not let the basket pass judgment first, since it is the best criterion?' The answer to this, which is reason enough, is that you run the risk of losing a pigeon once you race it, then you are back where you started. You have lost the bird because you had no confidence in its pedigree, and you have to begin all over again.

Let us assume that a pigeon which you consider a good one turns out to be an unsuccessful racer. Are you going to get rid of it or give it another chance by breeding from it? I certainly would not dispose of it. Once the bird has been tested by the

The selection of breeding stock

basket, whether successfully or otherwise, it will only cost you another year to try it out on breeding.

You may have heard of cases where one of two nest-brothers turned out a crack flier while the other's performance remained mediocre, and later the crack proved a mediocre breeder while his 'useless' brother produced outstanding offspring. I came across a similar case in the loft of Franso van Immerseel at Keerbergen, where I tried to judge the performance of the two brothers by their appearance but failed.

Quite frequently, it happens that a top flier produces mediocre offspring, but that this offspring in turn breeds outstanding youngsters. It is all a question of how favourable a combination of hereditary factors a bird is given, and how many of the factors that have been recessive in the previous generation (according to Mendel's laws) reappear in the new generation. A pedigree keeps its promise, unless the pigeon grows up in an adverse environment and remains physically under-developed. I will come back later to the effect of environment on a bird.

Here is another golden saying from Louis Vermeijen, a point he always brought up during conversations, 'If you want to breed champions, keep down the number of old birds by racing or destroying them.' In other words, be careful what you breed from, or you will be sorry when it is too late. If a strange bird catches you eye and you buy it, put it in the breeding loft. But when it comes to the offspring, put them through the mill! If they are an asset to your loft, breed on. If not, get rid of the lot. That is the rule.

When I was introduced to the Huyskens-Van Riel team in 1947 I came away with a newly-laid egg from *Bliksem* (Lightning) mated to *Sproet* (Speckles). My *Jonge Bliksem* (Young Lightning) was a small, dark check cock. Everybody who saw him doubted his parentage and thought he looked more like a small hen. I knew his pedigree: *Bliksem* was the son of *Oude Witzwing* (Old Whitewing) and *Boerinneke* (Peasant Girl). *Sproet* was the daughter of *Bange* (The Timid One) and *Donkere Duivin* (Dark Hen). *Bange* and *Boerinneke* were brother and sister, thus the

The selection of breeding stock

pairing of *Bliksem* and *Sproet* was close inbreeding. It was on these two pairs that Huyskens and Van Riel based their successful post-war breeding. *Jonge Bliksem* was mated to *Blauwe 590* (Blue 590) from my own stock, the best young hen to emerge in the difficult races from France.

Testing your pigeons in head-wind races is indispensable, for even a dud can win with a tail wind, and it is wise to take into account when judging the performance of a pigeon you intend to breed from all the conditions of the race: distance, temperature, wind direction, whether it pulled away from the 'drag'. A prize won in a test flight is only of value if the pigeon has had to contend with every imaginable difficulty. A race where everything goes wrong, on the other hand, gives no clues whatsoever. It is of no value as a test.

Jonge Bliksem and the *Blauwe 590* were a breeding pair, and this illustrates my principle, which I never abandon. Wherever I go, I always stress the vital importance of this system. If you buy a new pigeon, you do not race it, you do not even train it. You give it a mate that has proved its worth. One of the youngsters produced by this pair was sold to the United States to Dr. Whitney who was so impressed by it that he immediately got in touch with me. Ever since then we have had a lively correspondence and Dr. Whitney has twice been my guest.

Another youngster from the pair went to Louis Vermeijen. He advised me strongly not to race the first-born cock produced by *Jonge Bliksem* but to keep him solely for breeding. I like to follow the advice of experienced people. You are never too old to learn. The following year *Jonge Bliksem* came in from the fields one day and died in the loft of chemical poisoning. This was a great tragedy, but I still had his eldest son, named *Willy* after Franz Huyskens' son, and later referred to as *de Oude Willy* (Old Willy) everywhere in the pedigree. He deserved a good hen. There were plenty of young hens in my own loft, but I decided against close inbreeding. My friend and neighbour Louis Pepermans had a blue cock among his youngsters who caught my eye. He was a son of *194*, who had won first prize from

The selection of breeding stock

Doudan for Sundays running. Judging by this youngster there ought to be something good among the next round. And there was. I took a blue hen and named her *Blauwe Pepermans* (Blue Pepermans). True to my principles, she never saw the inside of a basket, for I knew her pedigree. Her father, as I have said, was *194*, her mother a hen called *Jonge Ster* (Starlet). *194* had been sired by *Goede Blauwe* (Good Blue Cock) from Van de Weyer's loft, mated to *Kleine Cattrysse* (Small Cattrysse). The blue Van de Weyer had won pools of 100 in the Haacht Federation. He had been bought in a total auction of the Van de Weyer loft after the death of its owner. The Cattrysse hen came from Diksmuide, from a brother of the Cattrysse of Moere in Flanders. This pair has been the basic breeding pair for Pepermans' line breeding.

What do we find on the mother's side? The *Jonge Ster* hen was the offspring of *Jaarling* (Yearling), a half-brother of Pepermans' *Goede Witzwing 1947* (Good Whitewing 1947), and the hen *Oude Ster* (Old Star) of Huyskens-Van Riel. Louis Pepermans had chosen her during a visit he and I had paid to Ekeren-Donk to pick a youngster which Louis had acquired from Jef Van Riel in an auction at the champion show at Contich. Now Jef Van Riel had bought *Oude Zwarte* (Old Dark Cock) when the Jaak van Dinter loft was sold. The hen we picked from a large number of youngsters happened to be daughter of this van Dinter cock.

I want to break off here to ask the reader whether he has noticed—and he should have done if he has read this record of ancestry carefully—that all the mating in this pedigree of the *Blauwe Pepermans* have been crosses. From which he must not deduce, of course, that either I or Pepermans pair *all* our birds on the cross basis.

I have not told this story without a reason. It is a deliberately-chosen example which shows how much inportance I attach to pedigree. I could equally well have picked an outstanding youngster produced by inbreeding.

The thing to remember, therefore, is this—if you want to be a

The selection of breeding stock

successful breeder insist on a first-class pedigree, a pedigree with a row of brilliant racers or parents of brilliant racers, a pedigree which is made up of a series of pigeons with excellent flying qualities, in other words a large number of favourable hereditary factors. Louis Vermeijen called this 'a kind of cross-breeding which isn't really cross-breeding but inbreeding of hereditary factors which are "related" to each other in so far as they are all favourable.'

I paired two pigeons which I intended to form the basic breeding stock for a line. My expectations were not to be disappointed. The progeny was good. Two of them, the *Zwarte Willy* (Black Willy—6181333–52) and the *Blauwe Witzwing* (Blue Whitewing—6181338-52) were stocked without ever having seen the inside of a basket. This proves that one need not hesitate to stock a fine youngster without a test, if its parents have a good pedigree and have previously produced good racers.

Here is another example—in 1952 I decided that I could do with another late-bred hen from Pepermans' loft, then at Zemst. Louis had 41 late-bred youngsters. All were to be sold straight from the loft one Sunday in October. On the Saturday before I was to choose my hen. But I declined. I said I did not want first choice; I would be satisfied with what was left. Why not? The youngsters were from the best breeding hens and the widower cocks which had proved outstanding racers in the preceding season. Since I knew the loft, the pigeons and the owner, I was quite confident that nobody could predict which of the youngsters would make the best breeding stock.

I assisted the purchasers in their choice, consulting the stud books as I did so. I was left with the *Geschelpte Pepermans* (Blue Check Pepermans—6066849–53). When I looked up her pedigree I found that she was inbred. Her ancestors, both on her mother's and father's side, were the *Goede Blauwe* Van de Weyer cock and the *Kleine Cattrysse*. She was given for a mate the outstanding cock *Ezemael*, which for eight years had been the fastest short-distance racer in the district.

3
The breeding system

So now we have the pigeons we want to start with, or continue with, as the case may be, the pigeons we want to race and use for breeding. We will not keep these particular birds forever, of course. Experience will show which of them are worthless. Some will be lost in races or in some way, and even the best ones will die one day. We therefore have to make sure that there are others to take their place, and, what is important, take it in good time. In other words, we must breed youngsters, we must pair our pigeons. How do we go about it? The simplest way is to let each bird choose its own partner, to let them mate freely.

Louis Vermeijen believed in 'free mating'. He was the promoter of this controversial system, and—whatever others may think about it—he has applied it to his loft with great success. However, I am not saying that he let all his pigeons mate at random. Whoever knew him knows that he regarded his pigeons as experimental material. He went about the sport in a scientific way and like any scientist he had his field of research, in his case pigeons. This is why he was generally recognized as an authority on the subject of pigeon racing. He could write and talk about pigeons with conviction, because he could draw on personal experience. You will hardly find a book dealing with pigeon racing in a scientific way which does not mention the name of Vermeijen. Not all his pigeons were allowed to pair up as they wished. But if, at any time, he was faced with the dilemma of not being able to make up his mind, he said, 'I am going to let

The breeding system

the birds decide.' The widower birds never had any difficulty in deciding. Some pigeons have an affinity with each other, a mutual attraction stemming from a feeling of being similar, of belonging together.

I have known him release from their loft the hens he wanted to pair with the widower cocks and let them swarm into the widower loft. Some hens immediately found their partners from the year before. The novice cocks descended to the loft floor amidst the blustering hens. Within minutes every nest box was occupied by a pair and courtship could begin.

'Now I challenge anyone to come along and tell me he gets better breeding results with any other method,' Louis then used to say.

I have discussed this system on several occasions in *De Duif* and can only repeat what I once wrote, 'Only the man who has a first-class breeding stock and a bit of "pigeon wit" about him can afford to do this.' Louis Vermeijen and his loft in Mariaburg fulfilled both conditions.

You may call this method of breeding 'too simple', but it is certainly a method of selection. Many fanciers would see an improvement in their lofts, a positive measure of success, if they became surer in assessing their pigeons and had the strength of mind to do away with any bird below average. The remaining pigeons would naturally possess the best combination of favourable hereditary factors, and the result would be what we are aiming at—the best mated to the best.

I do not know whether anyone else in Belgium or abroad follows this method, but I have applied it repeatedly to my widower birds. It is the surest way of getting good racers. At least I think so. With widower birds the rule is (and it is as well to remember this) that it is the right hen that makes a successful cock. Birds that are allowed to pair up freely will perform better than those that are mated against their will.

Against their will? Indeed, this does happen. You give a cock a first-class hen, with an eye to valuable offspring, and you find that the cock's racing performance drops far below what it used

The breeding system

to be. He dislikes the mate that was forced on him. As soon as he is given back his former mate, he improves. He recovers his former courage and zest. This shows that even pigeons have a will of their own. We may call it a whim, but it is more than that.

Usually, though, a fancier does not let his birds pair up freely but sticks to the old method. In autumn or winter he draws up a carefully considered plan which he subsequently changes more than once in attempts to improve on it. What should he do—cross-breed or inbreed?

Before I go any further I ought to explain a number of terms which have become part of the language of breeders, although they are scientifically wrong and could lead to misunderstandings.

The animal kingdom is subdivided into phyla or sub-kingdoms. One of them is that of the vertebrates, which is again divided into classes. Within the class of birds, our racing pigeons belong to the order of pigeons. Each order is subdivided into families, each family into genera, and each genus into species. One of the species of the genus wood pigeon is the rock dove, *columba livia*, the forebear of so many strains of domestic pigeon bred by man. One of these domestic strains is the racing pigeon.

For ages man has tried, through selective breeding, to obtain strains of domestic animals with permanent hereditary qualities. A strain is made up of all animals with certain marks or features, attributes or qualities in common. To the expert these are a guarantee of the purity, the pedigree of the animal. If pure strains are paired they pass these distinctive features on to their progeny. If two birds of a strain of domestic pigeons are mated their young will exhibit the features of that particular strain of pigeon.

The breeding of racing pigeons is so advanced today that they have become a definite strain with permanent hereditary characteristics, in which the colour of the feathering is of no consequence. The only important thing is their ability to return home from any distance, no matter in which town, country and continent they are hatched.

After having defined the term 'strain' I want to say a word on

The breeding system

'cross-breeding'. In strictly scientific terms cross-breeding only defines the mating of two animals belonging to two different species. Consequently we are using the wrong term when we speak of two pigeons from different lofts which we have mated as being 'cross-bred', because they are both of the same species.

It is in Belgium that breeders started to pair (not to cross) birds of two types. The types were called the Liège Pigeon and the Antwerp Pigeon. The breeders paired, raced, and selected them; they brought in new birds from good lofts and acquired a reputation for the performance of their pigeons. Terms like Vermeijen strain, Huyskens-Van Riel strain, Cattrysse strain, etc. were born. This is breeders' language. It came about because the large, successful lofts, by thoughtful breeding, turned out definite types that were immediately recognizable. It would probably be more accurate just to refer to 'Herman's Pigeons', or 'Bricoux Pigeons' or 'The pigeons of Havenith-De Fayter', etc.

Pigeon breeders work on two systems, cross-breeding and inbreeding. Neither of them, as far as I know, has ever been used in a loft to the complete exclusion of the other. In some lofts we find a clearly separated combination of both systems, but in most lofts it is a combination with a great number of variations, applied at random according to circumstances or the owner's fancy.

Yet cross-breeding and inbreeding are the subject of endless discussions over which gives the best results. They have always been the bone of contention among theoreticians. Everyone has his own arguments and examples.

What do we mean by cross-breeding? It means the mating of two entirely unrelated pigeons. The term also includes the mating of two pigeons whose pedigree shows no common parentage for five generations back. What is inbreeding? There are several nuances to the term, such as breeding in and in, close breeding and line breeding, varying from the closest form to relationships of the fifth degree and over. We should be careful when talking of inbreeding, since it can mean so many different

The breeding system

things. It all depends on the degree of closeness with which the birds in question are related.

When we hear of someone who has been closely inbreeding his pigeons for years without their showing the slightest signs of deterioration, someone who breeds exclusively from his own pigeons without ever introducing a strange feather into the loft, then we ought to take it with a pinch of salt.

Most pigeon fanciers' magazines outside Belgium advertise pigeons for sale which are of Belgian stock. No wonder. Belgium is the leading pigeon-racing country in all the five continents, but there are fanciers everywhere who can compete with the best among the Belgian fanciers. What surprises me is that we in Belgium seem to be less talented in the art of breeding. Outside our borders there still exists the 'pure' sort of breeder that died out in Belgium half a century ago. As far as I know there are no 'pure' offspring left in Belgium today of the stock of these once-great fanciers. It seems that fanciers outside Belgium manage to breed on and on without ever importing a foreign feather. I do not know how they do it; in fact I venture to voice some doubts.

What is the situation in Belgium? In the German paper, *Die Brieftaube*, Ewald Bäumer writes about the Janssen brothers at Arendonk that 'for 25 years they have not introduced a single strange feather into their loft'. That *may* be possible. But it need not necessarily be so just because a foreign paper prints it. The Janssen brothers are top-class breeders and realistic enough to realize that it is impossible to survive for so long without introducing some new blood. In *De Duif* of 15th April 1959 I wrote, 'I recently read in a report in a Brussels newspaper that the Janssen brothers "occasionally add some of the best to their stock" '. Not 'often' or 'never', but 'occasionally'! Perhaps we ought to interpret it to mean 'in good time'. I do not see how they could otherwise have stayed at the top for so long. When I read this account in the Brussels paper I said to myself, 'Well done, at least they are honest!'

I once heard the same thing said about Franz Buelens from Malines, namely that he bred purely from his own pigeons.

The breeding system

Franz never dreamed of such a thing. When I first visited him, along with Louis Vermeijen, I discovered in his loft a bird from Torrekens, a dark cock with many white feathers. And later Buelens admitted to us, 'Of all the pigeons I have added to mine, the ones I bought from Jos Van den Bosch at Berlaar are the best.'

'Well said,' I thought, 'at least he is honest!'

Buelens later on bought some more birds from another top loft. And why shouldn't he? How else could he have held his position in the Malines clubs year after year from 1923 and at the same time sell good breeding and racing pigeons?

A reporter from Brussels once wrote of Boeykens at Bornem that he had several times sold all his pigeons bar two and then made a new start with this one pair and had still remained champion. I suggest that the reporter did not understand the Bornem Flemish. If you told people in Klein Brabant this they would laugh their heads off. I published this in *De Duif* too, and nobody protested. Our breeding methods in Belgium differ quite considerably from those employed by many breeders in England and the United States. We constantly combine crossbreeding and inbreeding. In England and the United States fanciers prefer inbreeding because they set great store by the purity of the great Belgian strains. They know all the names of the great Belgian breeders whose experiments have made history. It could be said that with them it is the label on the bottle that counts.

How about Belgian breeders? I quote Dr. Whitney in *The American Pigeon News* of October, 1961:

'My impressions of pigeon racing in Belgium? The thing I consider most interesting is this: while we in America show great reverence for the famous old strains, the Belgians are much less concerned. My friends in the States would be delighted to be able to show someone a Bastin, Wegge or Hansenne pigeon and say that it was pure bred. In Belgium there is scarcely a fancier who knows there are any Bastins, Wegges or Hansennes left. And this is the country where pigeon racing origina-

The breeding system

ted! Most of the fanciers whom I had the honour to meet have heard of these famous names, but they do not attach as much importance to them as we do. They will say that competition was not so keen in those days and that a racing system was used which the masses did not understand. They will say that because of this pigeons were rated more highly than they are today when everyone applies the widowerhood system. Belgian fanciers are in pigeon racing mainly for the profit. Their aim is to breed pigeons which will make money for them. They do not favour close inbreeding but they do like to take an inbred bird and cross it with the best among their own birds.

'They show less interest in pigeons of the old strains which had a name in the past. What they are interested in is the pigeon of today which helps them gain a reputation, trophies, money.'

Dr. Whitney wrote this after his four-week stay in Belgium. I have shortened the article.

The question is, are we behind the times when it comes to breeding pigeons? Let us look at the question more closely.

In the same number of this American magazine I found a Chicago breeder advertising pigeons for sale. What was he offering? Wegge pigeons from Tom Buck in England and Putmans in Ireland, an old Belgian strain via foreign breeders.

What happened in the past and is still happening today to the best of our Belgian pigeons? They are sold by their original breeders to various lofts abroad, then these lofts, in turn, sell pigeons to other lofts—not the original Belgian ones, but pigeons that have been bred from them. But is it not conceivable that some breeder abroad who has bought pigeons from a Belgian loft has some to spare and re-sells them to another loft abroad? Besides, foreign lofts have, at various times, exchanged Belgian pigeons among themselves. I ask myself, without any suggestion that these transactions were done in anything but an honest and regular fashion, 'Who can guarantee that all the pigeons in the foreign lofts were strictly inbred?'

If a fancier, on successive occasions, buys pigeons from a breeder in his own country and breeds solely from these pigeons

The breeding system

and no others, can he then say that he has been exclusively inbreeding? Certainly not, for the breeder from whom he bought his original pigeons does not concentrate exclusively on inbreeding. The purchaser does not acquire pigeons which are all closely related to one another. The breeder does a good deal of cross-breeding, and there is not the slightest doubt about that.

Whenever a total or partial sale of early or late-bred youngsters is advertised, details are always given of their origin and ancestry. We always find that the breeder has bought strange pigeons for cross-breeding or exchanged birds with friends. Whenever I brought up the question of cross-breeding versus inbreeding during my visits to large lofts, in conversations with reputable breeders, I was always told that close, uninterrupted inbreeding is impossible without occasional cross-breeding to improve the strain. Breeders have also told me that they know of no one who could stay at the top without alternating between inbreeding and cross-breeding.

Drawing on scientific writings, on my own empiric observations and on advice from the best breeders, I will try to show readers the best way. I would like to start with a quotation from *La Selection Animale* by Louise Gallien, published by Presses Universitaires de France (page 75):

'The mating of close relatives, if continued indefinitely in one and the same line, tends to bring out pure, recessive lethal factors which are the cause of weakening, declining vitality and decreased resistance to certain diseases in pigeons.'

In *Evolution, Genetics and Man*, Dobzhansky has this to say,
'Darwin showed long ago (1877) that plant progenies obtained by self-pollination within a flower, by cross-pollination of different flowers of the same plant, or of different individuals of the same strain, are deficient in vigour. They suffer *inbreeding degeneration*. Conversely, the progenies obtained by crossing different strains exhibit *hybrid vigour* (or *heterosis*, as it is now called).'

He says further,
'The geneticist, G. H. Shull, found that inbred lines, obtained

The breeding system

by systematic selfing, rapidly dwindle in vigour, size and yield of the plants. Intercrossing *different* inbred lines gives progenies in which the vigour is restored. . . .'

We cannot do without theories, but experience is still the best teacher. Experience cannot be disproved. There can be no argument, as there can with theories, over whether it is valid or not. With a theory you plan something, and if the plan can be turned into reality, the theory is valid. You have then done something which works and can be referred to on future occasions.

If the pigeons in a loft have been closely inbred for so long that they all resemble one type, it is high time something was done about it. Their performance may still be good but it will not remain so for much longer. I am not talking here of 'inbreeding' but of 'persistent close inbreeding or breeding in and in'. Besides, I am speaking exclusively of pigeons. There is a danger in reading something on heredity, on genes and chromosomes, pure lines and strains which are uniform in all factors, and applying it to pigeons. It is bound to work, we say, it has to work, because the theory says so!

In No. 4 of the Dutch racing pigeon publication, dated 26th January 1961, I found a very interesting article by J. G. Pluym entitled 'Problems of Heredity'. The author seems to have absorbed a great deal of theory, but he has remained sober and factual for he does not cling blindly to words but acknowledges reality by referring to experience and facts. I am not going to quote the names or the sources from which he derives his theories, but I will quote his views in the following lines, which coincide exactly with my own views,

'Are not the laws of heredity the same for all animals? I do not think so, but if we want to breed pigs that give more meat we try to breed longer pigs. Both long and short pigs are equally easy to fatten, but there is more room for meat between the legs of the long type.' However, where pigeons are concerned, we are not looking for one or two features only but for a whole complex.

The breeding system

Anyone may doubt my ability to tell a chicken from a pigeon, but there are others whose words carry more weight. Pigeon fanciers can always benefit from wise words, especially those of someone as experienced as Dr. Bom, a physician who was a well-known personality in Dutch pigeon racing circles. It remains true that 'the racing ability of a pigeon is due to many factors, most of which we do not know. Nor do we know how these factors are related to each other'. I would like to point out that these are Dr. Bom's words, not my own.

For the most part, we are groping in the dark when we try to discover which characteristics we have to breed and secure in our pigeons. We know only some of them. If we say of a pigeon we are holding that 'this is going to be a good one', we are often misled. Everthing still depends on a healthy upbringing and the test of the basket.

I love to hear people talk of 'pure-bred by persistent close inbreeding'. It sounds imposing.

I have read (and this fact has also been quoted by Mr. Pluym in his article) that the progeny of rats produced by persistently mating brothers and sisters still showed no trace of degeneration in the 50th generation. And Dr. Dobzhansky states that the phenomenal improvement of the yield of maize in the last two or three decades has been obtained by the introduction of hybrid corn, but the hybrid seed must be obtained from systematically inbred lines.

Is this not exactly what Dr. Whitney said in his account of the breeding system preferred by Belgian fanciers? Belgian fanciers are not out to advocate either inbreeding or cross-breeding, nor, for that matter, a combined system. Their only interest is in breeding pigeons that fly hard and regularly win top prizes, and this is achieved by thoughtful inbreeding and cross-breeding.

Some say that racing is not an end in itself, but a means of selection. The aim is a high breeding standard. Let us not split hairs. A high standard of breeding has been reached when the pigeons are highly successful as racers.

We can do nothing without inbreeding, because it is in this

The breeding system

way that certain good points can be selected and fixed in a strain. But if we want top racing ability we won't get any further unless we apply judicious cross-breeding. Successful cross-breeding relies on previously successful inbreeding. Inbreeding first, cross-breeding second—that is the recipe for high-performance pigeons. I cannot emphasize this enough.

Cross-breeding will in many cases lead to greater variability, although there is certainly a danger of some qualities being lost. But 'it is by virtue of this variability that super-cracks can be bred', Mr. Pluym says. I would like to add that the result of cross-breeding will be less variable if the two types to be crossed are essentially similar in build.

My aim, then, is judiciously to combine both systems, inbreeding and cross-breeding. In doing so I am following Vermeijen's theory and practice, namely to inbreed and occasionally cross-breed with a strange bird which is as close as possible to my own pigeons in ability, character and outward appearance. Vermeijen called this 'inbreeding of qualities'. The beginner must start off with valuable birds of first-class breeding. After stringent selection he will discover whether they come up to expectation.

What do most of Belgium's top breeders do, the ones who have remained in the lead year after year? They look for outstanding material to cross with their own, for birds which by their appearance, performance and pedigree are at least as good as their own birds, or preferably even better. Then the new acquisition is mated to a good bird of their own loft which has been more or less inbred. I agree with Mr. Pluym, 'A strain can only be improved by cross-breeding with another strain of equal or superior quality!'

Inbreeding by itself improves nothing. Youngsters which match their parents in appearance and characteristics need not be equally successful. We certainly cannot expect inbred youngsters to surpass their parents. A barrel can only yield what it contains. What is more, if we concentrate exclusively on inbreeding we can be sure of retrogressing.

When I aired these views recently to a small circle of fanciers,

The breeding system

one breeder made the following appropriate remark: 'This is all very well, but don't forget that all you have just told us is nothing but theory. In practice things look different. Spend large sums on buying pigeons? Only a certain class of fanciers can afford that. The large masses cannot.'

Without doubt there is a good deal of truth in his words. Everything is difficult in the beginning. If you have no pigeons you have to find a way of getting some. If you have been in the sport for a little while but have had no success you must start all over again, but if you have been in it for quite some time you just have to try to keep your head above water. Well-bred pigeons naturally cost money. I must add one warning, though. It does no good to hurry things. A beginner or run-of-the-mill breeder would be well advised not to indulge in extravagances which are the privilege of the professionals. It would be foolish to go for birds from top lofts right from the start.

In nearly every small village in Belgium there are one or two lofts which are above average and whose performance is not to be sneered at. No one will go bankrupt if he obtains some eggs or young birds from these fanciers. After all, this is only the beginning. Later on we can go one better. Our motto should be *excelsior*, higher and higher. But we cannot get to the top in a day or two. Beginners would do well to remember this unless they want to be prematurely discouraged, in which case they would have done better not to start at all.

Once a fancier has got to the point where his pigeons win prizes in local races against pigeons from the same district, he can consider that he has made more than a satisfactory start. I have noticed, however, that at the auctions held at most pigeon shows, pigeons are sold off far below price, much to the disgust of the donors, who feel offended. Fanciers who, because of their business connections, give away a dozen or more pigeons a year, are naturally pleased if they get a high bid.

I know of a case of a young fancier buying four late-bred youngsters for 1000 francs (about £8 10s.). He then asked the breeders for advice on how to treat the birds. The breeders were

The breeding system

so pleased that they took an interest in the young fancier. Doesn't everyone feel flattered if someone shows more than a casual interest in his pigeons? This young fancier confided to me later that one or two breeders had invited him to come again for an egg or a youngster, and they also said that if he was unlucky with the birds he had just bought, they would soon find replacements.

I am not saying that this happens every day, nor that it could happen with every breeder. I am simply mentioning this episode to show that it pays to keep one's eyes open on championship days. The small fancier with limited means can always find something here.

In Antwerp, Boom, Lier and Malines, every year early in spring, country boys, whose pigeons have open loft all through the year, offer young birds for sale on the market. (This is a common practice in Flanders.) The boys never put pigeons in a race. They have only one aim, pocket-money for fun. Wherever early-bred youngsters are offered for sale, whether it be in an auction or from individual lofts, excellent bargains may often be found. There are frequently some outstanding birds among them.

Don't turn your nose up at these pigeons which are sold in open markets. They are not sold for the table. Fanciers from Southern Belgium and from beyond the borders come to Antwerp and Lier markets. They must be doing well out of it, for they return every year. I have watched them examine the youngsters to see whether they were healthy, whether they had strong bones, sound feathers, and a clean throat. Initially all youngsters bought in this way should be trained. The ones that turn out well should then be left at home, while the others carry on. I would be quite satisfied if they won nothing, but returned from a 200-mile race fresh and unspent. After the moult I should sift them mercilessly, mate all the yearlings the following year and race them in widowerhood on the second round of youngsters. I might even go to the market a second time. In that case I would certainly look out for the breeder who sold me the best youngsters the year before.

The breeding system

But I have no illusions, far from it. It would probably take me three or four years to get anywhere. But then, I daresay, I would make the grade.

The lads at the market do their best to breed pigeons that can compete and will fetch a good price. You may laugh, but I have seen one boy at Boom produce prize lists to convince the buyer and push up the price of his squeakers.

I hope nobody will misunderstand this little diversion, but I think it is justified. After all, I am not writing for one particular category of fancier; I am writing for everybody, and that includes the small fancier. I am not saying that pigeons bought at the market are necessarily the answer for everyone. I am only saying that if for any reason you cannot afford to buy expensive pedigree pigeons you will have to make do with a small number of good ones, whether you buy them at an auction or at the pigeon market early in the year. You never know.... You would not be the first, nor the last, to try again and again until eventually he got hold of a genuine, top-class racing pigeon, either at the market, or at an expensive loft.

Let me summarize by quoting Vermeijen once again, 'Mate the best to the best.'

The fancier tends to think that by 'the best' we mean the best racer. Well, I have nothing against this; in most cases this will be true, but strictly speaking the best breeding pair is the one that hatches the best young. They may be good fliers or not. For this reason, a newly-acquired pigeon is usually given a new mate after a year's trial. The new mate may result in better offspring. If this is so, then the pair stay together. If not, we revert to the first pairing.

Vermeijen says, 'If a pair breeds well, leave them together.' As far as I know his two outstanding breeding pairs, *David* and *Dikke* (Fatty), and *Agent* (Bobby) and *Rosse* (Sandy) stayed together throughout their lives. And why not? It is foolish to go on experimenting. If something is good it should be left at that, or the good may be undone. However, any pair that breeds rejects should be separated.

The breeding system

A pair does not always produce offspring of uniform quality. Influences beyond our control may make the quality of the youngsters vary from season to season. This is as true of the whole of the loft as it is of one pair. But variation in quality does not mean that only rejects are produced in any one year. The progeny of good pigeons, if it is healthy and developing well, deserves to be given a serious test. Only when it then does not come up to a certain standard can we speak of rejects. Remember, however, that it has certainly not been proven that both parents are to blame.

If you cannot make up your mind which birds to pair together, let the birds decide. It will save you a headache, and after all, we do not really know anything about it ourselves. We can only wait and see what emerges. Remember that a pair which produces nothing but good youngsters, and among them perhaps a crack, is an exception that even the great lofts may have to wait for for years.

New stars rise and set again in the sky of pigeon racing. A star often owes its rise to the lucky combination of a breeding pair, but just as often the breeder is back to where he started once that pair has left the loft.

I have already dealt with some of the mistakes which lead to a rapid decline. I have talked repeatedly about persistent, uninterrupted inbreeding. Now I want to say a word on occasional close inbreeding.

It can happen that for some reason or other a fancier loses one half of his best breeding pair or that he wants to go the whole hog in applying the theory. He then pairs up father and daughter, mother and son, or brother and sister. Does this work? Why not, provided that he does not try it with birds that have some kind of fault or shortcoming, because that would certainly go wrong. The two related birds must, above all, be one hundred per cent healthy and physically perfect.

Since nearly all pigeons, unfortunately, suffer from some minor if not major fault in conformation, there is always the danger that this fault will be accentuated in the young, and that

The breeding system

would be fatal. Anyway, if you *do* get healthy youngsters from a mating of this kind, the youngsters should be mated in turn to entirely unrelated birds which are free from this fault. Under no circumstances should you continue to inbreed. You are bound to fail—always. Nor should you expect one bird of a pair to compensate for the faults of the other. It would be wrong to mate a very small bird to a very large one in order to breed pigeons of medium size. Similarly, if you want a pigeon's offspring to have more back it would be wrong to mate it to another bird with a hump back. An attempt to create improvements in this way violates the laws of heredity. It is a fallacy to think that two extremes will cancel out each other.

The safest way to correct faults in offspring is to mate the pigeon that has the fault to one which is perfect in this respect. This promises the best chances of youngsters which are free from the fault. They may not all be, but there is always a chance. Do not expect too much! In nine out of ten cases a closely inbred mating of this kind will not be successful. But do not pronounce failure hastily, either. Healthy youngsters must be given a chance (I cannot repeat this often enough) as youngsters and yearlings!

Finally I would like to tell a story:

Some years ago Louis Pepermans confided to me that he was not satisfied with the youngsters of three closely-related pairs. He usually applied remote inbreeding, but in the case of these three pairs there had been no alternative. An untrained eye could not have detected any signs of degeneration, but then degeneration was not really the word for it. When I asked him what it was he disapproved of, he replied, 'The youngsters are a bit below par. I think they are too refined; they have no drive, no guts. They come in well up the field, but they cannot win first prizes like the others. I shall have to have a look round for something new.' He took the first opportunity that offered itself, and at the auction sale of the late Dorsan Naessens' loft bought the well-known *Vooruit* (Vanguard) and *Oude Donkere* (Old Dark Check). From Vereecke in Deerlijk he bought *Atomic* and *Jonge*

The breeding system

Hengst (Young Stallion). By cross-breeding these four pigeons—and another youngster from Tournier at Lommel—with his best breeding stock he gave his loft the *coup de fouet*, the crack of the whip, as Guillaume Peeters from Biomont used to say.

He did not have to wait long for success. He went from strength to strength. In 1962 his loft, which had been attracting the attention of Belgian fanciers since 1947, reached an all-time high.

Inbreeding—cross-breeding—strict selection—back-mating—strict selection—cross-breeding, this is the golden rule which can keep up the high standard of every loft and the whole sport.

4
The environment

One thing is certain: from a pigeon's egg only a pigeon will hatch, never any other bird.

The pigeon is distinguished from other species of birds by its outward appearance, by its own particular shape, the colour of its head, its eyes, its wings, its legs, etc. This outward appearance is called the phenotype. The hereditary characteristics of a pigeon, which are determined by the combination of genes in the egg, are known as the genotype.

It is important to remember that there is a considerable difference between the characteristics arising from heredity and those which are the result of environment. This is where we come to the term 'environment', which is of such great importance to us.

We have no control over what becomes of a pigeon as a consequence of its inherited characteristics. We have to wait and see and take what comes. A pigeon's genotype is more or less constant. Not so the phenotype. This is partly determined by heredity, but for the most part it develops through the influence of environment. 'The question, which of the two factors, heredity or environment, is the more important in the development of [the pigeon's] personality, is futile.' (Dobzhansky)

The outward appearance of any individual changes frequently. If you take your family album and look at some of your childhood photographs you will hardly recognize yourself. The differences in appearance between child and youth, youth and adult, adult

The environment

and old man, are due to heredity and to the environment in which a person lives. The same applies to pigeons.

How do we define 'environment'? When I asked one fancier he replied quite simply, 'Why, it means the loft.' But it is not as simple as that.

Environment means immediate surroundings, the surrounding region, objects and circumstances. In the case of a pigeon I would say it is all those factors which influence its development and performance in the place where it grows up.

When we breed two youngsters from a pair of pigeons, we know that they will not resemble each other exactly. They will differ in quality and appearance because the combination of genes in each one is different. If neither of the two is removed from its original loft, so that both grow up in the same environment (and provided that this environment is favourable to the development of the youngsters and their training), we can be fairly certain to end up with two good pigeons, despite minor differences.

But what happens if one of the youngsters stays while the other goes to another loft? How will the two compare after the moult, as yearlings, as adult pigeons, in five or ten years' time?

The greater the difference between the two environments the more noticeable it will be that one of the two looks better, has been kept better, shows less wear. This is because they have grown up in different surroundings and in different lofts, with different food, and different breeders. Their training has not been the same, nor the way in which they have been raced. The number of factors contributing to the complete difference between one pigeon and its nest brother, even as a yearling, are endless. We do not have to wait for the first signs of wear to notice the difference; it shows almost immediately, from the moment of separation, and increases steadily. And there is another thing.

Let us assume that four or five well-bred pigeons from different reputable lofts come together in a new loft. They all come from different environments to settle down in a new environ-

The environment

ment which is strange to them all. Don't expect them all to change their phenotype (their outward appearance) in exactly the same way. The better the environment from which they came and the worse the one in which they meet, the greater will be the difference in the way in which they adapt to the new environment. The greater their adaptability, the more quickly and easily will they grow up and develop. A pigeon's adaptability is put into its cradle, so to speak. The fancier can help the pigeon by making the environment more favourable and by making the bird resistant to changes in environment. It is a known fact that some pigeons adapt better than others, but it is very rare for a bird not to settle down at all.

It is no longer a secret that fanciers, when buying youngsters or breaking old birds into a new loft, take along some food from the old loft to make the change-over less abrupt. I can quote an example of this.

Some years ago O. De Jonghe from Wezembeek-Oppem made me a present of a two-year old hen. After it was mated and had settled down nicely, I freed it. It flew off in the morning and did not return till the evening, but it was never seen at Wezembeek. It was not until it had hatched its youngsters that it flew back to its former loft, twice every day. In the end it occurred to us that there might be something in De Jonghe's food which the hen wanted for its youngsters. I mixed some of his food with mine, and the hen 'deserted' no more.

A wise breeder will not change food suddenly, not even to keep birds in top form, and he will get in a large enough store of food to last the season. In my opinion this is proof that even such relatively small matters as food alter the environment and must be given close attention.

It is important for every fancier to create the right environment for his pigeons. He need not wrap them in cottonwool, but he should protect them against any influence that could interfere with their normal growth and development, unless he wants them to be prematurely spent. If a pigeon from Flanders is moved to the Ardennes or to Limburg, another one from inland

The environment

to the coast, what happens? Very often nothing. The pigeon shows no signs of strain; it possesses a good measure of adaptability. But this is not always the case. The fancier who fails to make allowance for the change frequently under-estimates a pigeon and culls it without having given it a chance to get used to its new surroundings. The bird is subjected to changes which the breeder cannot possibly prevent altogether, changes in climate and air, in the atmosphere, in food and, of course, in the breeder.

A pigeon is not likely to die, like a plant transplanted from its original soil, but we should try a slow, gradual transition, a carefully planned, methodical adaptation. The bird must be given time to settle in. It is often a good idea to cross-breed with an indigenous strain.

After a change in environment, it is common for a pigeon to fail for some time, to fall short of expectations. The breeder will have to be patient. It is often better to keep such a bird solely for breeding. The next generation or the one after that will most likely be back in form. At least the breeder knows then where he can buy pigeons that will adapt to his environment, and that is something worth knowing.

The most important thing for us is that we create as favourable an environment as possible to our pigeons. The breeder is the decisive figure in this game. Remember what Jef Van Riel said, 'It's 80 per cent the breeder . . . within six months he can have a good loft!'

Let us take a closer look at the various factors contributing to environment. First, the breeder.

The breeder must know how to get the best out of his pigeons. To do this, he must know them in general and every pigeon in particular. He must make a study of pigeon psychology. Psychology is the science of the human soul, in particular the soul of every individual. Although we are all human beings we all differ from one another. Our behaviour, our inner life is subject to fluctuations and changes throughout our life. We often say apologetically, 'Never mind, he is only a child,' meaning that when the person has grown up he will be wiser and act dif-

The environment

ferently. We also say, 'Remember he is an old man. What will they say about us when we have reached that age?'—the implication being that an old man cannot be made responsible for his actions in the same way as a man in his prime.

There is, then, the psychology of the child, the youth and the grown man. We also differentiate between the psychology of the masses and the psychology of the individual. Our mental life changes according to the circumstances we live in, according to whether we live alone or are in contact with many people. Our behaviour changes, and the same thing applies to all living creatures, pigeons included. Under certain circumstances pigeons react in one way; under different circumstances they react in another. They differ according to the way they have grown up, and they differ from one bird to another. A fancier must learn to recognize the reactions of his pigeons, to understand them and catalogue them, in order to determine whether or not they can be put to use.

We classify a pigeon according to its build, its skeleton, its balance. We judge its muscles, its feathers and wings, and we can tell from experience whether it will be a good racer and whether it will produce physically sound, good youngsters. But if judging a pigeon's build, its muscles and everything about its outward appearance was all, our job would be much easier. There is something else, something which lies hidden within the bird. This is why we study it, its behaviour, reactions, peculiarities. There is nothing a vet's scalpel could detect in an outwardly perfect pigeon which would distinguish the champion from the average racer or the dud.

'It doesn't work like that,' says the simple man, 'they've just got it in them.' And he is right. For a pigeon has a 'soul', which we can only understand if we come to know its intellect and character.

To be precise, a pigeon does not really possess either intellect or character. This is just breeders' language to describe the instinctive behaviour of our birds.

Human beings have intellect. We reason and think before we

The environment

act, but animals, pigeons, do not reason. Their actions are governed by inbred instincts. The laws of nature determine their behaviour, and they cannot escape these.

We know that every pigeon differs from the next. Not all of them are equally talented, if I may put it like that. Not all have equally strongly-developed instincts. We must look to the ones which have the most and make use of them. We must look for the pigeon's soul.

Let us be frank, we look first and foremost at the eye of a pigeon, the mirror of the soul, to discover what is in it and behind it. Like Vermeijen, I used to use a magnifying glass, but I have given that up. A magnifying glass shows us the physical structure of the eye as an organ of sight. It does not show us the mirror of the soul. So what good is that? Does a magnifying glass disclose whether we have a clever bird, or one with a strongly-developed homing instinct? We may even judge the bird worthless. Vermeijen says, 'Under a magnifying glass the general impression is lost,' and that is certainly true.

It is in the nature of man to reach for what is most easily attainable and first to arouse his interest. When a pigeon is still, lying motionless in our hands, its eye alone is moving. This in itself attracts our attention and interest, and this is why we look at the eye.

I would like to draw a parallel here—a portrait must talk to the beholder. The more the painter has managed to get away from the mere outward resemblance to express the soul of his sitter, which must be in his eyes, the more it does so. The portrait must be 'alive', we say.

Take a masterpiece of portraiture, Leonardo da Vinci's *Mona Lisa*, the woman with the enigmatic smile. I ask you, what is it that makes the Mona Lisa's expression mysterious? Her eyes, or the smile playing round her lips? Take a print of the portrait and cover in turn the eyes and the mouth. Then tell me where lies the mystery which has made the painting so famous; in the eyes or the lips? Is it the mysterious look or the mysterious smile?

When talking to another person we look at his eyes. We do

The environment

more than that; we watch the movements of his eyes, the raising of his eyebrows, the wrinkling of his brow, the movement of his lips; we listen to his voice, its volume and intonation. We watch the gestures he makes with his head and hands to emphasize what he says. We can tell a lot about the other person's state of mind from his manner, his behaviour. The eye is not everything, but it is the centre of attraction. Although we take in everthing that goes on around us in our field of vision, the eye attracts our main interest.

We scan everything as a television camera scans a scene, in order to transfer it to the screens at home. In judging the value of a pigeon, pay most attention to the overall impression. Of course, the picture a pigeon presents in a show cage is incomplete. It is altogether different from the one it presents in the loft, where the bird is seen in its usual and unaffected manner, driving, hatching or feeding.

Every pigeon behaves differently in different situations, even if a casual observer believes all pigeons behave alike. Their reactions differ in duration, intensity and effect. With a pigeon that is just coming up to form there are even more differences. There are an infinite number of signs which an observant fancier can come to recognize and which can tell him when he has to treat a pigeon in a particular way. After all, not all children of one family have one and the same character or react in the same way. In bringing them up and educating them the parents learn that one child must be handled with patience while the other responds to firmness. A child who is slow on the uptake needs more patience than one who is quick-witted. We find timid and bold, sentimental and hard, peace-loving and belligerent natures among pigeons just as we do among men.

It is here that the skill of the loft owner counts. He must be familiar with every pigeon and know how it reacts in certain circumstances, how it indicates that it is in form, what he has to do to improve and maintain it, in short, how he can get the maximum out of the pigeons he enters for races. Why do one man's pigeons fly straight through the loft window and into

The environment

their nest boxes (in other words straight into his hands) after a race, while another man's birds perch on the loft roof, wasting valuable minutes? It is a question of breed, says the second man, but this is not the case. It is a question of the breeder himself and the way he handles his pigeons.

In some cases the design of the loft, especially the trap door, is to blame. But after all, the loft does not just stand there one morning all ready built and unalterable. It is something which is built and developed according to the breeder's instructions and ideas. If the design proves unsuitable for his requirements, what is to stop him from improving it?

A pigeon must be brought up and taught like a child. In this connection it might be useful if I gave some hints that apply to all animals, but in particular to racing pigeons.

A pigeon has a lively temperament and is quick to learn, because it shows an intense interest in everything that goes on around it. It is not all that difficult to pick the best out of a flock of selected racers. It is the one which shows the greatest interest in the visitor. There may be pigeons in the loft which have beaten this one on occasions, but if we draw up a comparative list of performances over a longer period we will probably find that the most inquisitive pigeon comes out on top. Like most of its loft-mates it has experienced a great variety of things, good and bad, comfort and discomfort, successful and disastrous races. It has learned to adapt itself to all situations and knows instinctively and from experience how to react best to overcome danger. This bird is very quick on the uptake.

Anyone who wants to teach a pigeon something must apply skill and patience, and above all persistence.

Why skill? Because he has to choose the right way, the method that promises most success. Why patience? Because no one can expect to get anywhere with pigeons without having the patience of a saint. Why persistence? Because there are obstinate and timid pigeons. The way to tame them, to make them overcome their fear and to break their obstinacy, is hunger. Give your pigeons their feed in their nest boxes and remain standing there

The environment

until they come. If they don't come they get nothing. Hunger will have the desired effect in the end. The only way to succeed is to persist, without haste or impatience, until everything runs smoothly. The pigeon must learn that there is an intimate bond between it and the breeder, that there is nothing to fear and everything to be gained from a relationship of mutual confidence.

For this reason, it is better to leave the squeakers alone while they are in the nest and handle them as little as possible. Once you have separated the youngsters, get into their midst and teach them to feed by scattering the food all round your feet. They must get used to your hand. It is vital that you control your voice and feelings. Speak in a quiet and relaxed voice, but, above all, *do* speak to your pigeons when you are with them. Avoid quick movements, and when you want to get hold of a pigeon do so without haste and in such a way that it cannot escape. Never chase a pigeon. Get hold of a bird while it is in the nest boxes or feeding on the loft floor and is not aware of you. It is better to lose a second in trapping a pigeon after a race than to make the bird lose minutes in future races through your nervousness.

Once a pigeon has learnt something, it knows it for good. If it does not do what it has learnt it is the breeder's fault. Pigeons like routine; that is certain. Always let them out and call them in at the same time. Always use the same signal. Whether you rattle a corn tin, whistle or call does not matter, but you must never change the signal. If you do, you interrupt the routine and confuse the pigeons. They can no longer tell the difference, they hesitate and everything goes wrong. If this happens, it is not the pigeons but the breeder who is to blame.

No matter for what reasons you call your pigeons, be sure to give those that come first a treat, just a trifle, perhaps two or three grains of linseed or dari. Those that are last get nothing. Next time they will be quicker. This is the rule; the one that does well is rewarded, the one that fails is left out. If you show determination, even if it means that some birds miss a meal, you will

The environment

eventually teach them obedience. They won't come to any harm.

But if a cock returns late from a race, unplaced, because the distance or the heat was too great, or the weather was foul, or whatever the reason may be—in short, if everything was against him—why should he not find his mate in the nest box? Why deprive him of something he has been promised, which is right, which he needs to spur him to do his best? This would be punishing a bird that did not deserve punishment. You would only discourage it, and that discouragement would be the reason for the next failure.

And if a pigeon has deserved to be punished? Well, that is a different matter. Here is a true story:

I know a small breeder in Oelegem, a simple man who is neither a university graduate nor a businessman; he is a postman. I am referring to Jules Tuyaerts, a tree of a man with mighty fists and a resounding voice, who manages to win firsts in the Antwerp Union and championships in the Eastern Federation.

I don't know any other breeder who handles his pigeons so calmly and considerately. With his calloused hands he handles them as tenderly as a mother her newborn. Tuyaerts had a widower cock, a very fast Quievrain racer, who had his nest box immediately opposite the loft door. Every time Jules came into the loft the bird started to spin like a top. He always had something for all the pigeons, a kind word, a pat, a titbit. The *Fast One* failed several times without a definite reason. He could and should have won. Jules decided to teach him. The bird knew that he always found his hen waiting for him whether he was fast or slow. Why should he hurry? For over a week Jules remained steadfast: The *Fast One* got nothing, not one friendly word, not one treat, nothing. He had to sit and watch his master treat all the other birds as usual. After a few days he cooed and turned no longer, but sat motionless.

After two weeks, Jules relented. On Friday night, the day before the birds were to be basketed, he came to the loft and treated the *Fast One* like all the others. The bird was beside him-

The environment

self with joy over the unexpected change and followed his master all over the loft. 'I believe he will do it now,' Jules said, 'I will stake him for all I have.' He came first with a two-minute lead in the St. Quentin regional race.

That is a true story. Of course, not all of us are breeders of Tuyaerts' calibre. The *Fast One* was later stolen from the loft, together with the whole breeding stock. But Jules did not take long to make up for the loss. He is still one of the most successful short-distance fanciers in the Eastern Federation.

The story illustrates some of the points I have made. It shows what is meant by a close bond between breeder and pigeon, and how pigeons have to be treated to get the best out of them.

If you don't keep your head, you throw away your chance of prizes. You can get further with less trouble if you go about it the right way, with patience and self-control.

An observant breeder will not be slow to realize that he can often improve matters by altering some small detail in his loft. Vermeijen thinks that a true breeder ought to be hammering around in his loft every season, either for the good of the pigeons or for his own amusement.

For example, the closer the pigeons are to the breeder the easier it is to tame them. If widower birds have to fly two or three yards from the entrance window to the nest boxes they tend to be shy. They are more difficult to catch. In some lofts the widower cocks as well as the hens enter the loft through a trap where they can be caught. It is quicker this way and there is no danger of one bird flitting off outside and detaining the new arrivals on the roof.

I did not have a large entrance in my loft at Puurs, but I never had any trouble. Everything always went as smoothly as clockwork.

5
The loft

Quite frequently fanciers who want to build or alter a loft send me letters with plans and drawings. They do their best to make it all very clear so that I can see what they are aiming at. They want me to comment on whether their plans are sound, and if not, want to know how they can improve them. Sometimes I cannot make head nor tail of their descriptions and drawings. It is enough to make me tear my hair out, and yet the matter is so ridiculously simple.

I have seen palatial lofts, and lofts made from bits and pieces, spacious lofts and 'dolls' houses', lofts in the attic, over outhouses, in gardens, and wall boxes for a few fast short-distance birds. They were all good, because they met the most important conditions—they were healthy lofts.

Which are the conditions that a loft must fulfil if we want to keep our pigeons healthy and, provided they have it in them, get them to race successfully?

A loft must have sun, light and air. It may be cool or warm, depending on its kind, but it must be bone dry, free from draughts and protected against sudden and drastic changes in temperature. If top-class pigeons fail to race successfully, the loft is frequently to blame. Not every fancier can build himself a loft as and where he likes. We do what we can. Not everyone can house his pigeons in the attic, even if an attic is much to be preferred to a garden loft.

We just have to give the problem a bit of thought. If we don't

The loft

find the best solution immediately then experience, a look round the neighbour's loft, or an old hand's advice may bring a turn for the better. Not everybody can have his loft to face in the right direction in relation to the prevailing winds, but this is very important in a changeable climate.

In my first book *Gij en ik over duiven* (*You and I on Pigeons*) I wrote that my loft at Malines faced due north. My pigeons had to fly in through so-called drop-holes in a wind-deflector, which kept out the cold and wind. In the loft itself not a breath of wind or draught could be felt. Under the drop board there was an opening through which the birds could enter the loft. There was hardly any morning sun, but the south side of the roof had glass tiles. The cold north wall was left clear of nest boxes, but it was insulated. It was a good, healthy home for the birds.

But I had not worked out this solution in a single day. To start with, I measured and calculated and recorded temperatures at different times of the day and year. The loft was cool and dry. The ceiling was wire mesh over which, in winter, sheets of hardboard were placed as protection against the cold. The loft was not ideal, but it was good. I exploited whatever possibilities it offered. I must add that my own and my neighbour's chimney went through the loft, which was no small help in keeping out the cold and damp.

The sun, the life-giver, provides warmth and light, but it gives much more than that. Nowadays, the sun and its rays are very much at the centre of scientific interest, and modern technology has made intensive research possible.

Our lofts cannot do without a great deal of sun and light, but we must avoid too much glass, which leads to abrupt changes in temperature. For example, when the sun goes down, glass dissipates warmth quickly, cooling down the loft very suddenly.

We let our birds out daily, not only to exercise them but to give them the benefit of the sun. Many fanciers exercise their birds around midday when they get the most sun.

To keep the widower cocks quiet, the loft can be screened. Not completely darkened, just screened against excessive sun-

The loft

light, no more. If you watch your birds, young and old alike, in and out of the nest bowls, you will find that they turn towards the light like house plants. Let them benefit from sun and light as often as possible.

Some fanciers are known to keep their pigeons in the dark to delay the moult as long as possible and race them with complete flights. But this is interfering with the normal course of nature and I would not recommend it. The birds will later moult quite abruptly to make up for lost time. One day they will sit there almost bald, and it will be an excessive strain for them to cover themselves up again. Instead of the slow process of a normal moult, they are faced with the sudden replacement of their feathers all at once. This necessarily takes much more out of them. It is certainly not conducive to a good moult, for each feather, whether big or small, must get its full complement of nourishment. The quality of the feathering is bound to suffer. Besides, there is the danger that during a sudden change in the weather the whole flock will start to sneeze. Then we are faced with them sitting there in their inadequate plumage, and there is no telling what the consequences for the following season might be.

No pigeon can be expected to remain healthy if there is no oxygen in the loft, no change of air. There lies a problem—how can we provide fresh air without draughts? Whether the roofing tiles are sealed or not is of minor importance. Sealed tiles do not make the loft unhealthy, nor do loosely fitted tiles, with the moon and stars shining through the gaps and the wind whistling through them, make it healthy. Instead of tiles, corrugated asbestos sheeting can be used, but then an additional ceiling must be fitted below this. In any case, there are better materials than ordinary roofing tiles for providing the loft with fresh air and replacing used-up oxygen.

The following arrangement is usually found in better lofts: fresh air enters through openings at floor level in the front of the loft. It rises at a fair distance from the birds' heads to the top of the back wall. In other words, there are ventilation holes in the bottom of the loft front and in the top of the rear wall. Whatever

The loft

way the holes are arranged, they must be so made that the circulation of air can be adjusted. In the Huyskens-Van Riel loft both intake and exit holes are at the top. Jef Van Riel considers this system best because there is definitely no risk of draughts.

It does not matter which material is used for building the loft and its interior, as long as it absorbs moisture. A fancier friend of mine, who is a cabinet-maker, built himself a model loft. He told me, 'There is nothing like wood, but it must be bone dry and free from smell'.

In all lofts, both the stock and racing pigeons live in nest boxes. This does not necessarily give them a draught-free home. What happens when the used air above the pigeons' heads rises? Does this not cause a draught? The answer is to have a dowel or wire grid above the highest nest boxes and place a false ceiling on top of this. I must emphasize again that it must be of moisture-absorbent material.

Why a double ceiling? The lower one is fixed and takes up about half the ceiling space of the loft. The upper one slides onto it and can be adjusted to reduce the gap through which air can circulate up into the roof. In severe cold and heat the breeder must decide for himself how far he should draw out or push back the upper ceiling, which serves as a regulator. The pigeons always sit under the lower, the fixed ceiling and are never exposed to draughts.

In a well designed and managed loft the difference between minimum and maximum temperatures is negligible. There is nearly always a thermometer hanging up, which is consulted regularly.

If the loft is too low to allow a second ceiling to be fitted, a protective covering at least should be fitted against the rafters. This can consist of sheets of hardboard or, better, chipboard and saves the birds from sitting immediately underneath the roof where they would be unprotected against extreme heat and cold. The air between the roof top and the hardboard serves as an insulating layer between the temperature inside the loft and the outside temperature.

The loft

I must repeat, pigeons must have a dry home, the air must be dry. Warmth is not necessary since pigeons don't mind the cold, but it does help their growth and offers the best guarantee of a dry atmosphere. The rule is, no matter whether it is scorching hot or freezing cold outside, it should always be better inside the loft. You should never be able to tell from your pigeons' plumage that it is raining or damp outside. If you have managed this, your loft is in order, you can adjust it perfectly to the weather conditions. This is not always easy. Not all lofts lend themselves to it, in particular garden lofts, but even in a garden loft we can do something to banish the worst enemy of health and good conditions—damp. But as I said, attic lofts are preferable. Very often they have chimneys from kitchens and living rooms running through them. It is well known that bakers are often the most successful fanciers. Their pigeons live in the most favourable conditions. This does not mean that I am against garden lofts on principle. Many a fancier with an attic loft wishes his pigeons were racing as well as those of a colleague who has a garden loft. But any garden loft that is successful is well designed. Care must be taken not to leave an open space under the loft through which the wind can whistle. The walls should be insulated cavity walls. In this way, the loft will meet the basic requirements as satisfactorily as any good attic one.

There is one big advantage the garden loft has over the attic loft. The house is ready built and the direction the loft faces cannot always be chosen, but with a garden loft it is easy to select the best direction.

Fanciers with garden lofts often have to wait until far into May before they send their pigeons to races, but this is no drawback. There are plenty of attic lofts which do not start before May either, and that is soon enough. If you start later, you race longer. Those who start earlier often have to stop just as the best races are coming up.

It is surprising how some lofts that seem to violate all the rules of good design nevertheless get good results. I deliberately said 'seem to', because the breeders know they are running a

The loft

risk, but they are clever and resourceful enough not to let the shortcomings become a danger.

I have read somewhere that a loft ought to be hermetically insulated. I don't agree with that; what we want is a slow air change, no more, but that does not mean that the loft must be a windowless box. The size of the loft and windows must be in the right proportion to each other. There must not be too much glass, but not too much insulating either.

In the first half of July 1963, we had some exceptionally warm days. They had been long in coming and brought unusually high temperatures for our region. It was not really too warm, but we had not been used to it for a long time, nor had the weather been conducive to growth. Fresh winds had made the nights too cold. When there was no wind the air became saturated with humidity. Dry warmth is the ideal pigeon weather. Damp warmth spells the outbreak of diseases in our lofts.

Dr. J. P. Stosskopf, veterinary surgeon and author of an interesting brochure called *Diseases among Pigeons*, who writes regularly for a French pigeon racing paper, gave his views on 'Warmth' in an article in June 1965. I always take a lively interest in what vets have to say on pigeons and their diseases. They are specialists, and we can but learn from them. Plenty of other people read the article, and it led me to a discussion with a fancier who wanted to harden his pigeons. 'They must be able to put up with heat and cold, dryness and humidity,' he said. 'It makes them resistent. We can do without coddling.'

He carried his 'hardening' so far that I dared not enter his loft without a cap or hat on. It was as draughty as a church belfry and I told him so. He laughed. Then he quoted Dr. Stosskopf, 'Last week we saw that warmth encouraged the outbreak of *coryza* (cold) in a loft that has never been affected by it. The draught was not to blame, but the microbes, which could grow nicely in the warmth, certainly were.' So the fancier's conclusion was, if draughts do not encourage *coryza* then draughts are neither dangerous nor harmful and my pigeons must be able to tolerate it.

The loft

I showed him Dr. Stosskopf's article written the week before. He said in it that pigeons should not sit in a draught, and the change of air in the loft should take place over their heads.

Vermeijen, his successors and many racing-pigeon journalists, have always advocated a slow change of air. Most lofts have followed their advice. Dr. Stosskopf says that pipe or cigar smoke must disappear quickly. I have always held that it must dissolve slowly to indicate that there is no draught. Our views may differ here, but I am not sure. Maybe the doctor means that the smoke must not linger and would consider my 'sluggish dispersal' fast enough. It may be a question of interpretation.

On the other hand, Dr. Stosskopf may prefer a cooler loft. I am all for warmth. Jef van Riel's loft is cool, Sus Peeters' attic loft used to be warm, but both lofts were healthy. Jef's pigeons are outstanding short and long-distance racers; Sus concentrated almost exclusively on short distances, except for the odd race from Angoulême or Bordeaux for an old veteran that was about to be pensioned off.

I always say, 'Keep your widower birds in a box.' Jef Van Riel does not agree with me. 'Dangerous,' he says. I admit it, but there was always a slow change of air in my 'box', I made the test with my pipe. My opinion is and always has been, fanciers must be able to realize that draughts are dangerous and should be avoided like the plague.

Whenever I am at the seaside I go swimming, no matter whether it is calm or windy. Without drying myself I play with my grandchildren, but I have never yet caught a cold. This is because the temperature is constant and my body is cooled off completely by the wind. The wind is blowing, but there is no draught. If I open the door to somebody when other doors in the house are open, I run the risk of catching a cold. There is no wind blowing, but I have caused a draught.

In Kamiel Dierck's loft at 29 Berkenstraat in Malines the pigeons do not sit in a draught. They sit in the wind. The wind can blow into the loft from all sides, but the pigeons are perfectly healthy and race exceptionally well.

The loft

Emile Matterne of Overhespen has given over the whole of the first floor of his villa to pigeons. Since his occupation prevents him from cleaning his loft every day he has adopted the 'dry droppings' method. In rainy weather all the windows along the front of the loft are left wide open and the wind blows in, sometimes quite violently, but there is no draught. When I visit this loft I leave my hat downstairs. I have never caught a cold there.

I think I have made the difference between fresh air, wind and draught sufficiently clear, and hope that the reader will understand what I mean by 'keep your birds in a box'—sorry Jef.

To conclude the chapter I would like to say this, it is certainly not true to say that only the ideal loft can keep a pigeon healthy. It can be equally healthy in a loft which does not meet all the requirements. Pigeons are quite tough. In fact, they are very tough, as anyone will admit who has seen as many healthy pigeons as I have in lofts of which I could only say, 'How is it possible?'

However, it is no longer enough today to keep pigeons healthy. There is no doubt that a pigeon may win its prizes because of the class it is in. Class is an important factor, but form is more important. No loft can be called good until it is so designed that it enables the fancier to get his pigeons into form no matter what kind of season it is, no matter how bad the weather is.

6
Feeding

De Duif has published two booklets which have gone into several editions. They deal with the question of feeding and are called *Food and Water* and *Feeding, Food, Vitamins and Pigeons*. They were written by my editorial colleague Arie van den Hoek, who is an expert in these matters and a successful fancier. These two booklets ought to be part of every fancier's library.

My views in this chapter coincide exactly with those of my colleague. They are my personal views, the fruit of years of experience of big and small fanciers with whom I am in daily contact. They are not based on theory, although I have nothing against it. The knowledge we gain from experience is practical, real. Theory is confirmed or disproved by it.

The feeding of pigeons is an art, but it can be learned, and it is worth learning. Too many lofts make mistakes in feeding. When breeders then find they fall short of their goals, they wrongly blame the pigeons, the loft or some other thing.

The most important thing about pigeon food is quality. This must be the first consideration. Always feed *sound, sun-ripened, fully-ripened and matured* seeds. While any of these four qualities is important in itself, a good feed must combine them all. If one of them is missing, the food is incomplete, to put it mildly. The breeder therefore should learn to judge grains and seeds before he buys them.

Whether you buy the different types of food separately or as a

Feeding

mixture, have a good look at the displays in pigeon food shops. Different qualities are kept in different boxes or dishes. By comparing the cheapest with the most expensive you will learn to tell the different qualities apart. Pigeon racing is an expensive sport, but doesn't the cheapest often turn out to be the dearest, especially when a lot depends on it?

The best quality food need not always be the most expensive. Some fanciers have to see the season's results before they agree with me. The observant fancier sees it at once from the droppings of his birds, but it is undoubtedly better to learn to read the message in the food before you are forced to read it in the droppings. I once conducted an experiment by feeding four different qualities of maize to four different pairs. Their droppings decided which quality I stocked up with for the season.

Have a good look round and take your time. I eventually made up my own mixture which is probably better than that of most fanciers and certainly a few pennies cheaper. Why shouldn't everybody else follow suit?

Go for the most recent harvest, if possible, but be very wary of seeds that have only just come in from the fields. Young grain and seed is richer in nourishment but it must be stored and matured before it can be given to the pigeons. If the harvest has been brought in during showery weather (as it was in 1962), it must be stored for quite some time before it is suitable for feeding to pigeons.

Early in September 1962 I bought a quantity of fresh barley and wheat. The immediate consequence was loose droppings. This was not fatal, but I still noticed the difference in the autumn round of youngsters. This is the kind of thing anyone who knows anything about pigeons must notice. If just one variety in the mixture is below standard it may result in a whole season's youngsters or a whole season's racing being ruined. I don't think there can be any doubt about that.

Food which smells musty or has gone off, even if it has been washed, cleaned, polished or otherwise treated, can poison pigeons through the mould it contains. The older the food is the

Feeding

more it loses its nutritive value. It loses its ability to germinate, and the vitamin content decreases. It may even become entirely useless. Very often this is due to the way it has been stored.

The second essential requirement is the food must be complete. It must be a varied mixture providing the pigeons with everything they need. The ingredients of the mixture must be in established proportions to each other. The question of whether pigeon food should be varied or simple, light or rich, could be discussed from now until doomsday. Everyone insists on his own point of view. Varied means the mixture of a large number of different grains and seeds; simple, the combination of only two or three. Rich food contains a large proportion of legumes (beans, peas, tares); light food comparatively few. The amount, kind and quality of the nutritive and other components varies from mixture to mixture. The more varied the mixture the more likely it is to provide a complete and balanced diet. Legumes are richer in proteins than cereals. Therefore, a larger proportion of legumes make the food richer.

In his booklets, A.v.d.Hoek deals with this problem at great length. If I still had pigeons myself (unfortunately this is no longer possible) I would give them the most varied mixture I could find. I would make a thorough study of their food. The best is only just good enough.

Whenever anyone asks me for advice on pigeon food, I never give him the recipe for the most varied mixture but only for a relatively varied one. Why? Because the selection of legumes and cereals is a very delicate task. It only needs one substandard variety for the birds to lose their form. For this reason I would not like to be responsible for another fancier's choice.

I think it should be obvious whether beans, peas and maize are sound and well-matured or not. What about wheat, barley, tares and other small seeds? Well, I would not like to look too closely! Sometimes I shake my head when I see what young country lads, who have grown up among the stuff, feed their birds. I have grown old in an office, but they could learn a thing or two from me. In most cases it is probably negligence rather

Feeding

than ignorance. 'Surely it doesn't matter all that much,' they say. It is unbelievable.

'Why grey tares,' somebody asked me the other day, 'aren't the black ones any good?' 'Maybe,' I said, 'but they are washed, dyed and cleaned. They cannot be healthy. I don't trust them.'

In fact, the pigeons' droppings confirmed this. Sometimes I try to convince people with my tongue in my cheek by saying, 'When I was out to find a wife, was I wrong to look for a girl who wasn't painted?' They promptly give up feeding tares altogether, both grey and black ones.

It is possible to argue about the relative value of rich versus light food. Some lofts race well on one, some on the other. I am in favour of mixed food because this is how I feel it ought to be, and anyone who knows anything about pigeon feeding uses it. I have never read a book by an expert that did not advocate a varied mixture, and I have noticed that most fanciers follow this advice. I do not favour heavy food because the birds do as well, if not better, on light food. I have experimented to find the mixture that would give the best performance and have ended up with the lighter mixture. Dr. Stosskopf does not believe in feeding 50 per cent legumes; he advises 30 per cent.

Why am I against a heavy mixture? Because I do not believe in a theory that does not match up exactly to reality, that is disproved by practical experience. But is it possible to race well on a heavy mixture? Of course; I have always said so and never claimed the opposite. I have seen it work, but it works equally well the other way, and I have reason to believe that the birds have more stamina.

The Peeters-Beaufort team at Biomont was one of the best over long distances, and I have never seen heavier food anywhere else. Even the winter mixture contained a much larger proportion of legumes than our ordinary breeding and racing mixture.

The late Guillaume Peeters said, 'Any pigeon who cannot put up with it can go and choke on it, for all I care.'

This caused Louis Vermeijen to reply, 'Then quite a few will choke on your heavy diet who deserved better!'

Feeding

This conversation took place during one of our last visits to Biomont. Peeters shrugged his shoulders but, nevertheless, lent a willing ear to what Vermeijen had to say on pigeons and pigeon racing.

No one could come and say that the Cattrysse brothers from Moere, who feed large quantities of maize, could not match themselves against the Biomont team. It is senseless to compare the two lofts. Let us just say that two of the most successful fanciers in our sport hold completely contradictory views on feeding.

I agree with the Cattrysse brothers, and so did Louis Vermeijen. Nobody could say that his pigeons at St. Mariaburg were fed on a light diet, but it was not heavy either, especially after his acquaintance with A.v.d.Hoek from the editorial staff of *De Duif* had contributed to making it a bit lighter. Vermeijen, the grand master, is the one who said, 'What do we know about a pigeon?' He never considered himself infallible.

'I agree,' says Dr. Whitney. 'I consider a light diet better, not least of all because it is cheaper.' That is a point worth considering. The majority of fanciers cannot afford to spend money with both hands. They must scrimp and save to make ends meet. So why have expensive (heavy) food if cheap (light) food is adequate?

I believe that pigeons fed on a light diet have more stamina. Their bodies have less work to do. Don't we feed them on a light diet after a race, in several instalments, if the race has been a tough one? We do this so that the digestive organs are not overloaded and the entire body can have a rest.

Dr. Whitney says this:

'In many books and articles where the feeding of pigeons is discussed one finds statements to the effect that flying uses up protein and high protein diets are necessary. This is really not the case, as will be obvious when we realize that the energy for muscle contraction is derived from glycogen (animal starch) which is stored in the liver as glucose.

'This is what happens during muscle work: in the muscle

Feeding

there is a sugar/phosphoric acid combination (hexosephosphate), which acts on glucose when no oxygen is present and forms lactic acid. This occurs during each muscle contraction. When the muscle is relaxed there is a pause called the recovery phase. At this time oxygen is supplied by the blood and about one-fifth of the accumulated lactic acid is oxydized and used as fuel to resynthesize the other four-fifths back to glycogen.

'If too much lactic acid accumulates the muscle enters into a state of rigour, and when oxygen is admitted the lactic acid disappears. Fatigue is due to the increase of lactic acid. In endurance tests with animals it was found that those given sugar can perform three times as much work as they are capable of when on an ordinary diet.

'The racing pigeon is sent to his liberation point and in the shorter races starts the race empty. His muscle energy must be stored in his liver, blood and muscles. He is fed generally before the long races and digests food as he flies, using its energy for flying.

'He can use the protein, too, discarding the nitrogen in his urine and burning the remaining part. And fat can be utilized also, but neither fat nor protein is used until the glycogen reserves are spent. The fat is oxydized and burned before the protein, and the muscle tissue itself is last to be used. Very likely a pigeon would be exhausted and quit flying long before his muscle tissue was called on. What makes the bird lose weight in a long flight is the loss of water, glycogen and fat, all of which he can replace. Some protein is needed for muscle repair, but certainly on the basis of what is known about muscle food, protein is least necessary for flying.'

So much for Dr. Whitney. These are very learned words, but then Dr. Whitney is a learned man. I will say the same thing in simpler language, which will be easier to understand:

When a pigeon is flying, its muscles are working. They need fuel in the same way that a motor car needs petrol. Fuel creates energy. In the case of the pigeon the fuel is glycogen. This is why the food mixture must consist largely of those seeds which, when

Feeding

they are digested, produce the most glycogen, i.e. those that are richest in carbohydrates. We put a large proportion of maize into the mixture because maize is particularly rich in carbohydrates and the best energy producer. Fat, too, contributes energy, but oil seeds are of secondary importance, since other food-stuffs contain fat in sufficiently large quantities.

Proteins, or albumenoids, which are contained in large quantities in the legumes, are mainly body-building foods. They are used in making and replacing muscle tissues and feathers.

Proteins, carbohydrates and fat are found in all seeds of which a mixture can be made up. It is logical that we should choose those varieties which are particularly rich in what the pigeon needs, but that is not enough. The ingredients must be in correct ratio with each other. If we give too much of one or the other we upset the ratio. This is what happens if we feed too many legumes.

A mixture with about 30 per cent legumes is correct. If a fancier feeds only 25 per cent maize he has to make up the deficiency with other seeds rich in carbohydrates. He will get away with this in a mixture, but maize is by far the best. So why not feed 40-50 per cent maize in the first place, the way the best Flemish long-distance fanciers do? After all, they have done very well with this method.

When a fancier asks my advice I always try to make it as easy as possible for him by giving him the recipe for a 'basic mixture', which he can feed all the year through. He only has to supplement it according to the circumstances by making it richer (by adding more legumes) or lighter (by adding cereals). He can do this by adding peas or barley respectively.

The basic mixture is as follows:

5 per cent tic beans
15 per cent Tasmanian maple peas
10 per cent green peas
40 per cent maize
20 per cent wheat
10 per cent barley

Feeding

To make a more varied mixture, dari and sunflower seed (5 per cent each) can be added. The legumes can then (but need not) be supplemented by 5 per cent grey tares or winter peas. This mixture is based on the principles and tables of A.v.d. Hoek and on advice from Dr. Whitney. It has proved itself over many years and pigeons perform well on it, even over a distance of 615 miles. Don't let us forget the daily doses of 'titbits' Vermeijen recommends, a teaspoon of linseed, cabbage seed and canary seed, mixed together in equal parts.

Six small lofts I know at Puurs, where Sus Peeters, too, has his loft, feed the basic mixture plus titbits as racing mixture. On certain days this racing mixture is replaced by a lighter mixture, as is usual when widower birds return from a race. I shall have more to say about this in the chapter entitled 'Back from the race'.

The basic mixture is also fed in the off-season during the moult. The feed is then heavier, richer in protein. This is not because the basic mixture is adapted in any way, but because it is not interspersed with a lighter mixture. The moult calls for a rich feed because, in addition to having to renew their feathers, the pigeons must recover from a season of racing and breeding.

When the last but one flight has dropped, we change over to the winter feed, which means adding one part of barley to one part of basic mixture. The proportion of barley is gradually increased until the mixture consists of one part basic mixture to three parts barley. I do not think that this feed is too light; in fact I would not hesitate to increase the proportion of barley, especially during a mild winter. Louis Pepermans feeds as much as 80 per cent barley when he wants to keep his pigeons quiet, and wouldn't we all like our pigeons to perform as well as his do? The fancier can tell from the behaviour of his pigeons how much barley he ought to feed them. Pigeons react to sun and temperature. The essential thing is to keep them quiet.

I do not expect anybody to stick religiously to the mixtures as I have given them. A pigeon will not die or become ill if the mixture contains five per cent more or less of one or other variety. It pays to go easy on legumes, though.

Feeding

A fortnight before the mating time we cut down the barley content until we are left with equal parts of basic mixture and barley on the actual date. Pigeons need not be in form when they are mated. This is a fact taught by experience and passed on as a 'secret'. I, too, have abandoned the view that pigeons must be in top form at the time of pairing up. They must be healthy, that is quite enough. 'Thin blood', the unsophisticated country breeder calls it, and there are many shrewd breeders in the country from whom we can learn something. These are the men—and they do not all belong to the younger generation—who consider beans 'poison', and who have been in the front ranks of our sport for many years. They only race a few pigeons, but they win.

It might be argued that pigeons are in need of heavy food when they drive and tire themselves in this way. Maybe. It is a wise precaution to prevent them from exhausting themselves. This is best done by separating the hen in one half of the nest box and leaving the cock in the second, open half. This prevents fighting but it does not stop them from courting. They have time to eat and drink at their leisure. The proximity of the mate is enough to stimulate the hormone production, and that is all that is needed.

When they are mated and consider themselves as belonging together the birds must be allowed to fly freely, but it is not necessary to give them an open loft. They become too independent that way and in their excited love-struck frame of mind may become an easy prey to hawks, which are particularly active in the spring. If the birds are to be locked out of the loft then an hour per day is quite enough. They will not over-exert themselves during that time. When they come back into the loft each pair goes to its nest box. If there is any doubt about their willingness the fancier makes sure by closing the box behind them, providing them with food and water in the box. When the cock sees his hen in or near the nest bowl he will be less excited. This precaution also saves quarrels and fights and, later on, broken eggs. During the period of heat and jealousy, damaged feathers,

Feeding

pecked eyes and bloody heads are frequent and they can spoil a bird for the rest of the season.

When do we change back to the basic feed? We do that when the birds have been sitting on the eggs for eight days and are beginning to produce pigeon's milk, not before. In this way we make sure that they do not put on weight during breeding. It might be thought that this is a little late.

I once talked to an ornithologist about this question, and he said, 'We get severe winters here with plenty of snow and ice. Many of the wild birds die from starvation, but some always survive, and on the first of May they all have their eggs.

'This is just a saying, since we all know that birds do not stick exactly to this date. Their mating depends on whether spring is early or late. Whatever the date, nature is not bountiful at that time. It is not until later, when the young are hatched, that insects and caterpillars and all the nourishment that birds need are available in abundance, and that is exactly the right time. In spite of the thin time the birds have during the mating period they hatch strong and healthy young. And this is how it goes every year.'

I concluded from this that it is soon enough to start on the basic mixture when the pigeons have been sitting for eight days. As soon as the young are ringed, a handful of peas should be fed before the main feed.

I advise giving the youngsters a handful of peas before the main feed all the year round, until after the moult. They must get food which is richer in proteins than that fed to the old birds during breeding and racing. Old birds have to be *restored* or *recharged*. Young birds must be helped to build up their physique. Bones, muscles and feathers all need to grow, and grow fully.

If you re-read what I have said about the functions of the various ingredients essential to pigeon food, I doubt if you will find anything that can be left out. Of course, everyone ought to follow his own inclination, but I have always fared very well on this system, and everyone else who has adopted it has been

Feeding

amply rewarded. I must repeat, no one has to follow my advice as long as he adheres to the basic rules.

How much food should we give our pigeons? Assuming a pigeon gets by on an average of just over two pounds of food per month (I have read this often), can you be sure that this covers all its needs? If you take a pencil and paper you will find that this amounts to about 1¼ ounces per pigeon per day. For so-and-so many pigeons that makes so-and-so many ounces. Adhere strictly to that quantity, the books say. But are your pigeons to starve? Certainly not. So do not waste too much time calculating and measuring. After all, our appetite is not the same each day. One day we are so ravenous that we cannot get enough; the next day we pick at our food. Sometimes we don't know whether we are hungry or not; sometimes we blame the cold weather for our appetite, or the warm weather for the lack of it.

When feeding our pigeons we must keep our eyes wide open and observe very closely, for feeding pigeons is an art. It would be wrong to give them the same strictly measured amount of food each day. Not only do the birds not eat the same amount every day, they also don't take the same quantity of any particular seed variety every day.

Those who race by the widowerhood system can judge by the food that is left over and can be taken away; it makes no difference if each pigeon gets its food separately in its nest box or they all feed from the same trough. The difference in their feeding habits depends on the effort made during a race. It also depends on the day of the week. On the last days of the week the birds eat less legumes, but more maize, wheat and barley. The conclusion is that we should always give the birds more than they will actually eat. They will then eat according to their needs, guided by nature, by their instincts. If they are allowed to feed as they wish they will decide more effectively than the fancier what they want and need.

There is a limit to this, of course. A generous amount of food does not mean abundance. This would only lead to food being wasted, and it is too precious for that. The rule is that as soon

Feeding

as the pigeons start to drink they have had enough, and the food that is left over should be removed. Only barley might possibly be left.

Most fanciers make mistakes in weaning the young. Here are some tips on how best to go about it. The youngsters must be taken away from their parents after the morning meal. On the first day they are given only water, nothing else. On the second day they are offered a meal of peas, never small seeds. They must eat something which is worth the effort. For the following three or four days they have to learn to eat large seeds. Then they go on to the basic mixture, always preceded by a helping of peas. It is essential to teach them to drink. Just dip their beaks into the drinking fountain once, and the next time they will know. Some youngsters only have to see another drink to know how to go about it.

You can always tell a fancier who has failed to teach his young birds correct feeding habits by the state of his loft. Beans and peas are left lying around while the youngsters only search for the small seeds. The result is that their crops are only half full. Youngsters who have been trained to look for the large seeds grow much quicker in the beginning. The weaklings will be those who have been satisfied with the small seeds and have never learned to feed on the big ones.

All pigeons, old and young birds alike, must always show a healthy appetite at feeding times. As soon as they turn to the water container they have had enough. The food is then removed until they are next fed at the set time.

Pigeons like routine, in every respect. Youngsters with slack chests or vent bones that move back and forth under light pressure are suffering from a lack of legumes or sun or both. It may be that their parents did not get enough sun either.

All fanciers who are well-respected in the sport stick to certain principles, but they may apply them in different ways. And why not? Many roads lead to Rome. The important thing is to do everything thoroughly and at the right time, but the ideal system is to feed all grains and seeds separately.

Feeding

Not all fanciers can be expected to follow this principle; many do not have the necessary time. I saw this some years ago in Jef Van Riel's young bird loft. When I told Louis Vermeijen about it he was quick to reply, 'Champion pigeons are the exception, and so are master breeders.' The needs of pigeons change with their age and the seasons, with the phases of the breeding cycle, i.e. driving, incubating, feeding the young, and with the days of the weeks. We know that very well, but we must also act accordingly.

Pigeons also need grit and crushed oyster shells. Do not give them too much at once or they will descend on it greedily the first day and leave most of it the next day. I do not know why. Give them fresh grit every day, but in small quantities, and it will all go.

What about greenstuff, cabbage, lettuce, and so on? Yes, very good, but I would advise washing every leaf under the tap to get rid of the many insects that have been in contact with it and left behind dirt that might trouble the pigeons considerably later.

For the same reason, I would never advise giving pigeons grass to eat or letting them run free on the lawn. Only recently I have heard of fanciers having to treat their whole loft against worms before starting the season.

Factory chimneys and chemical fertilizers are other sources of trouble which you should steer well clear of.

Water should be plentiful and always fresh. In summer it should be renewed twice a day. It must be brought up to loft temperature and the drinking fountains kept scrupulously clean, inside and out. The water you drink yourself and use for cooking, whether it comes from the kitchen tap or a well, is the best to give your birds. Do not add anything to it unless there is a special reason.

I now want to add a few words on vitamins, primarily to warn the fancier.

I quote Dr. Whitney:

Vitamins. Another class of essential elements in food is vitamins.

Feeding

It may sound like heresy, but there is good evidence that far too much stress had been placed on this subject. Too many people drew rash conclusions from the scanty information available to them. We are now finding that we will need a great many more facts before we can speak with the confident tone many adopted some years ago. New vitamins are in the process of being tested daily, and there will be many others. Our knowledge will be incomplete and inconclusive for some time yet.

Vitamins are necessary only in minute quantities. With a few exceptions, all essential vitamins are present in the normal diet. When all our information is boiled down, it seems certain that pigeons can get all the vitamins they need from grains and sunshine, provided the proper grains are fed and plenty of time is allowed to birds to 'absorb' the sunshine, especially during winter months when the actinic rays are at a minimum. (*Keep Your Pigeons Flying, 1961.*)

It is true that the one vitamin deficient in grain is *riboflavin*. Pigeons that are prevented from eating young, growing grass or newly sprouted grains may show a deficiency and their eggs fail to hatch.

What does Dr. J. P. Stosskopf have to say on the subject?

'Both a lack and an excess of vitamins harm the pigeon. So far no one really knows how large a dose of vitamins pigeons should be given. It varies from pigeon to pigeon, depending on the state of the intestines, the presence or absence of parasites which interfere with assimilation. It also depends on the food a bird is given, and, furthermore, on the fact that an excess of vitamins in the blood is quickly expelled by the body.'

I have extracted this paragraph from *La Vie Colombophile*, where Dr. Stosskopf refers to his thesis, in which he pointed out that the difficulty of the experiment exceeded the technical means available.

What does Dr. Dobzhansky say in *Evolution, Genetics and Man*? He admits, with great regret, that it is quite impossible to improve anything with vitamins.

Feeding

Give your pigeons a varied diet of seeds, give them sun and give them rest, then you can manage without vitamins. If your birds are ill let the vet decide which and how many vitamins to give.

Is this all there is to be said on food and feeding?

I am not writing a book on the subject, only a chapter in a book. Therefore I will leave it at that. The point is, if a loft is racing well, then that is good enough. Anybody who wants to read more on the subject can do so in the publications I have mentioned.

7

Racing systems

Somebody who got wind of my intention to write a book on pigeon racing asked me if I would include some special advice on racing and racing systems. He said, 'That's what all fanciers are really keen to know—the best system, the system used by the great breeders.'

I replied, 'Sorry, old chap. The chapter on racing systems will be the shortest. Why should I waste twenty pages on it if less will do? How can a system help anybody?'

He seemed disappointed, but I couldn't help it.

From 1940 to 1944, in the main post-office in Antwerp, I taught a course in rationalization for young clerks about to take their second examination. One or two points I made then might benefit pigeon fanciers, too. What is rationalization? The definition we used at that time was: tackling a job intelligently, using common sense, getting the greatest benefit from the least effort, much of what is now known as work study.

What would you think of a car factory where every worker built a complete car by himself? You would think it idiotic, and rightly so. Cars are built on conveyor belts, every worker contributing to a part of the whole process.

What people have to learn are the laws on which the principles of rationalization are based, for they apply everywhere, even in pigeon racing. Here they are:

What is worth doing is worth doing well, and it is not the system that matters but the people behind it.

Racing systems

To make things very clear to my young colleagues I thought it a good idea to teach them to draw the right conclusions and to be able to deal with people. To this end I explained to them the basic principles of logic and psychology.

Logic is the art of drawing correct conclusions from the given data. Jan is a resident of Gent(1)—a resident of Gent is a Fleming(2). So Jan is a Fleming. Correct. That was easy. But take care: Jan is a Fleming(1)—a resident of Gent is a Fleming(2)— so Jan is a resident of Gent. That is incorrect! Jan might just as easily be a resident of Antwerp or Malines. He might, of course, be a resident of Gent, but this cannot be inferred from what has been said.

In the pigeon racing press, offences against logic are only too common. The fancier is blinded to the truth by irrelevancies. The majority of readers draw the wrong conclusions and find themselves deceived and cheated. It is just like a conjuror who does all sorts of things with one hand to divert the audience's attention from the other. A quick bit of finger work, a red herring is dragged across the scene—and everyone who knows nothing about logic falls for the trick.

Now a word on psychology in pigeon racing. A pigeon is more than just a bundle of feathers. It is a living creature which reacts on instinct. We can make it do what we want by getting it to react to certain signals. If we simply whistle to call our pigeons back into the loft, they do not realize what is expected of them. But if we give them a reward, something to eat or some titbit, they soon come to expect it and also to realize what they have to do to get it. We put a pigeon into the basket and expect it to return home as fast as it can, faster than all the other pigeons, if possible. To get it to make the effort we hold out a reward; when the widower cock returns home he finds his hen waiting in the nest box.

You know all that, you say. Of course you do, but the important thing is to know much more than your friends in the club, to be able to coax your pigeons to react to all kinds of orders and requests. It is these reactions that get them into

Racing systems

top form so that they fly fast and are keen to get their reward.

How you go about this, which system you use, is of little importance. It is not the system that matters but the fancier who is the most skilful, the most ingenious, for it is he who will get the most out of any pigeon. He is a top breeder.

What is a system worth?

During my student days I played outside-left on a soccer team. The team played on the one-two-three-five system. Then people started looking for a better formation, a better system. When I had long ceased to be an active player many clubs changed over to the attacking game. More goals had to be scored. And it worked. After a while the clubs realized that scoring a lot of goals was all very well but it was no good if, at the same time, their own team allowed a lot more goals to be scored against it. So they thought of something new, the blocking game, and that worked, too. When it was seen that the defence was still too weak, another improvement was introduced. The centre-half went back behind the two defenders, and, again, it worked.

At last someone hit on the idea that nothing could be as efficient as the magic square, made up of two inside-forwards and two wingers. Another new system, and it worked. It worked until Pele with his Brazilian team came along and played the rest of the world clean off the field with his four-two-four system. That topped everything.

Every system was succeeded by another which was the best until it was, in turn, replaced by something better!

If a team won on its system, the system was good. If it was beaten, the newspapers commented that the team had a bad day, their opponents were always seconds faster on the ball, etc, etc.

Pol Jacquemijns, our best-known football critic, once wrote, 'Every team plays the game which the opposing team allows it to play. To apply any particular system they must have good players.'

What he says here about soccer is, in fact, one of the principles of the science of efficiency, and it applies equally to pigeon racing.

Racing systems

It is not the system that matters. . . .

An expert racing his birds on the natural system will beat a fancier racing on the widowerhood system if the latter is only partially expert in his chosen system. A skilled operator of the natural system will certainly be able to hold his own against widowerhood fanciers, though not always, because his pigeons are not in form every week.

Now young men come along who want me to go more closely into racing and racing systems, because they, too, want to be among the best one day. The booklet *How We Race Them* (by L. Vermeijen and J. Aerts) tells you more than enough about it, and the rest cannot be taught. I will explain just one or two things, no more. Every fancier must find out for himself.

Youngsters are usually bred in December and ringed in January, so that fanciers can pair them before racing them. Yet there have always been late-bred, unpaired youngsters among the top winners of the National Young Bird Race from Angoulême, organized by the Cureghem Centre.

'This may be so, but paired youngsters nevertheless race better!'

Six or seven of us were sitting having a cool beer one evening. The fancier who said this looked straight at me. I only shook my head and said 'No!' There was a violent reaction from two others, but I kept quite. One of my table companions winked at me. Neither of us said anything. It doesn't usually pay to argue about such matters.

When my partner, Sus Peeters and I flew pigeons together we found that the young birds flew best if we kept cocks and hens separated for a few days and then let them mix five minutes before they were basketed. The two of us stood over them with a small stick to keep order. In the Quievrain race we finished up with seven prizes among the first eleven.

To separate the cocks and the hens we built a loft specially divided into sections. The first round of youngsters goes into one section, the second into the other. They remain there until the youngest can feed themselves properly. Then they

Racing systems

are all allowed to mix, but not for long. As soon as the young cocks start to coo and the young hens follow them round dragging their tails, the sexes are separated. They only see each other for a few minutes before being basketed. I challenge anyone to outclass them with paired youngsters.

This reminds me of a remark of Louis Pepermans' which made us all laugh. 'I am not suggesting that we like our wives any the less now,' he said, 'but let's be frank; when we were still courting we were keener, weren't we?'

With unpaired birds, we play on the attraction of powerful yet immature instincts. Later their affection becomes deeper, less turbulent, quieter. I can hear someone argue, 'But this only works once—or twice.' It is not the system, the widowerhood system, that matters, but what the fancier can get out of his birds.

Old cocks are raced on what we might call pseudo-widowerhood; they get their hen in the end. With young cocks it is one hundred per cent widowerhood. They are put next to an old hen sitting in the closed half of a nest box for a few minutes before being basketed. Young hens are raced on the natural system from August to September. The old widower cocks stop racing at the beginning of August. Laying and incubating do not take very much out of the young hen, and when it comes to feeding the young the old cock takes over the lion's share of it.

So you say it could only work once, or perhaps twice! Try it and you will find it works over and over again. It is our usual system, and it works very well.

The average fancier is very quick to accuse the successful breeder of resorting to 'pills and potions'. But the breeder who works in the way I have just described said to me, 'Publish the facts in your pigeon fanciers' press. The readers won't believe it. Those who do won't try it for that very reason. Even if some do try it, it is still highly doubtful whether they will be able to make it work, or whether they will stick to it until they can. After all, we have all had to learn the hard way.'

No matter what system you use, the pigeons must be got in form first. Sometimes a pigeon shows symptoms that indicate

Racing systems

that it is about to come into form. The fancier must be able to recognize them. He sees two or three straws or a feather in the nest bowl of a widower cock, and what does he do? He goes and cleans up the nest bowl and the whole loft. Why? Why doesn't he throw some nesting material on the loft floor? The pigeon's nesting has been aroused and is urging on the bird. Maybe other birds will follow it. This will not happen every week, but if it does, make use of it.

A good fancier notices such things, a better fancier does not; he does not wait to notice them, he makes them happen! That is the difference.

A cock leaves his nest box. He is looking round the loft to find a secluded spot. There is a little bench or a shelf in one corner where the clock stands on Sundays. He goes and sits in this dim corner, cooing softly to himself. Something is stirring inside him. What is it? An instinct awakening. Don't, under any circumstances, remove the bench or shelf.

Put something here and there in the loft for a bird to retire behind and dream. Leave a nest box empty for this or that bird to 'play at being master'. If you lose a pigeon, use the empty space to help a bird to get in form. Do not wait for the pigeons to show you. Make it happen! The thing to do is not to wait for something to stir, to become obvious, but to give the birds something or take something from them that will start up the reaction which puts them in top form.

All pigeons have different reactions, even those which seem to show a measure of similarity. Not all birds react equally quickly, equally strongly or equally long. Get to know your pigeons. You must find the best system and the best way of applying it. If it is your aim to get your pigeons into top form, you must avoid anything which might be harmful to form.

Beware of excessive draughts: a few air tiles on the roof is all that is needed for fresh air. They provide enough oxygen yet keep the warmth in. Above the pigeons' heads there is a ceiling, one half of which is movable. This serves as a temperature regulator. There is a double screen on the loft windows,

Racing systems

one of glass and the other of dowels, to control sun, light, temperature, and humidity.

There are fanciers who race well one year and the following year do not do well. There are other fanciers who race well one year, and the following year race just as well or even better.

The same breeder each year, the same system, the same loft, the same food, the same . . . No! different weather conditions. 'Different weather, different pigeons', the saying goes. This is true in most cases, but for the top fancier it must be 'different weather, same pigeons!' The man who wins prizes year after year, irrespective of the weather—he is the right man. Read again what I have said before and you will find the answer.

There is one more important element.

Food is of paramount importance. When the pigeons return from a race they are given a light diet. Why some people talk of a 'cleansing mixture' I cannot imagine. They probably mean well but use the wrong expression. Pigeons fed on a healthy diet need no 'cleansing'.

What do we give them? A mixture of barley, wheat, dari, sunflower seeds and some small seeds. The odd grain of maize will do no harm. They do not get much. Later in the day they are given a full meal. The food on the following days will depend on the circumstances. Was it a difficult race, a short, medium, or long-distance one, do the birds have to go back into the basket the following weekend or are they given a Sunday off? Is the weather hot, warm, cool or cold?

The less the effort and the warmer the weather, the longer should the change-over to the normal diet be delayed. I don't think I need say more. These few words cover everything one needs to know. If the birds are given a Sunday's rest the return to normal food is, of course, delayed longer.

The fancier must watch and see how his pigeons behave, which seeds they pick out of the mixture and which they leave. As I have already said, give them what they want. Give them more than enough. You can always remove what is left over to prevent them playing with it. Their instinct won't let them down,

Racing systems

but you will be wiser for it. In feeding it is not the system that matters but the How, What and When.

By giving his pigeons a well-designed loft the fancier keeps all harmful influences away from them. This and the food he feeds them helps them get into condition. By inducing certain reactions he stimulates them to attain their top form.

When is a pigeon 'in form'? What are the outward symptoms?

The skin on the breast must be clean, without scurf, but pink, or even red in the case of widower birds, as though the blood was flowing freely under taut skin. There is often a little red dot on the sternum. The eye cere and wattle should be chalky white. There is a definite brilliance to the whole eye. The eye-ball seems rounder than usual. This is because there is ample liquid in the space between the cornea and the lens.

The throat should be a light pink, the neck feathers shiny and smooth without 'plaits' in them. The wings should be held close to the body and the colouring of the feathers appear richer. The pigeon seems smaller and feels lighter when held in the hand. Its feet are dry, clean and warm. The tips of the flights have a slight bloom on them. The muscles of the breast are not loose but feel firm (not hard) and make the pigeon look rounder. The outer rim of the iris (if the bird has one) is shiny black.

A bewildering mixture of signs, all of them widely known.

The only important thing is whether the bird is in form and whether it is improving or declining. Put your pigeon into the basket and wait a few minutes. If it feels less firm when you take it out, something is amiss. In that case, you would be advised to be careful and not stake it too high. I know fanciers who leave a pigeon with these symptoms at home.

What are the signs indicating that form is improving? A bird has no sweat glands, but a pigeon that is really in form should feel slightly damp at the breastbone after it has been in the basket for ten to fifteen minutes. Push aside the small feathers on either side of the breastbone and you can feel it. The bird should glow when you hold it in your hand; it should seem to sweat.

Racing systems

If the pigeon brought up part of its last feed while it was in the basket, it is nervous, in super form. But you would be wise not to send it on a long-distance race that means it has to spend two nights en route. Put it in a short-distance race, or it might kill itself with nervousness on the journey. If the bird is eaten up by its nerves it will be tired before it starts.

8
The pigeon

This is a chapter on the pigeon itself. It will probably turn out slightly different from what most readers expect. I am not going to talk about the number of tail feathers, when the first of them is dropped during the moult, and which is the first and which the last to drop. Quite honestly, I have never been altogether sure myself, although I have often examined the tail very closely during and after the moult. I will not dwell on trifles here; they have been the basis for long discussion since time immemorial and probably always will be.

It is more important to know what the pigeon of today looks like, the pigeon that wins top prizes. Well, it certainly looks rather different from the one we raced half a century ago. The racing pigeon has undergone an evolution.

What is meant by evolution? A revolution is a complete, fundamental change. Evolution is a much slower process of change. Sometimes stretching over decades. It does not happen all at once, but gradually. Everything is in constant motion, undergoing constant change. Ever since it began, the world has been evolving steadily and we do not know what the outcome will be. The same has happened to our pigeons, is still happening, and will continue to happen. There is much discussion these days about whether the pigeon of today is different from and better than the pigeon of many years ago. It is certainly different in its phenotype, its outward appearance. When deciding whether it is better or not, many people say, 'The fastest pigeons

The pigeon

in the past were as fast as the fastest today, but the average pigeon of today is considerably better than the average pigeon was then.' I have no hesitation in suggesting that the best pigeons of the past would have to hide before the best of today.

Lofts are better-designed, food is balanced on scientific principles, racing systems have been improved, transport is faster and less tiring for the pigeons; fanciers are much more experienced and can get more out of their pigeons than the most eminent breeders of the past, and I say this without any wish to belittle their achievements, but there is something else. None of what has been achieved by present-day improvements, including training and cross-breeding, is hereditary. The favourable hereditary factors contained in the sperms and ova of parent pigeons can at best be preserved but never improved. It has been discovered, however, that over the years mutations have occurred. These are sudden, hereditary changes in the germ cells. This is the basis of evolution.

When a mutation was found to be detrimental it was eliminated, for who goes on breeding pigeons that are worse then their predecessors? When a mutation was advantageous, fanciers did not immediately recognize the cause of the improvement. They thought it was due to a lucky pairing. Wherever this happened the performance of the loft improved. Fanciers continued to benefit from the mutation (even if unconsciously), and over the years it spread over most of the lofts, as a result of selective breeding. The phenomenon became an accepted fact, which made Mendelism and its application to pigeon racing rather irrelevant.

Once again I would like to quote Dr. Whitney, 'Ever since man learned to write he set it down on record that like begets like. As Darwin stated, hereditary is implied in the term "reproduction".' Dr. Whitney scorns people who glibly talk about Mendelism without knowing the first thing about it. He says,

'Those who do understand Mendel's theory know very well that, as far as application to racing ability in pigeons, or horses, or milk production in cattle, or egg production in hens is con-

The pigeon

cerned, it is just about as much use as is water in one's boots.'

Why is it useless to apply Mendelism to pigeon racing? Because there is no single characteristic which makes a bird a better homer, of a faster flier, but rather it is the whole constitution of the bird.

'If we could say that a red checked pigeon flies faster than a blue check, then certainly Mendel's theory would be useful, and in a few generations we could breed out the blue check, because this difference is a good illustration of how Mendelism functions. Try to name any one physical feature which controls racing ability! You can't.'

The pioneers of our sport, the greater and the lesser ones, based their selection of pigeons on the birds' racing ability, without ever having heard of Mendel. They relied on experience, mated the best to the best and eliminated anything that could not win a race. Unwittingly, they benefited by lucky matings and favourable mutations of the germ cells as time went by. The old standards were superseded, evolution gave us better pigeons. Let the gullible ones continue their persistent close inbreeding without ever cross-breeding with a good strain from another loft!

What did we breed in the past? Heavy-duty racers, national champions, which were too lazy, too slow to race over short distances. They had to fly between 400 and 600 miles or more. They were released at one end and arrived at the other. Their chief merit was stamina. What do we breed now? Fast long-distance racers that can win prizes equally well over 60 miles or 600 miles. Not always, naturally. After all, I am talking about the élite of then and now.

Some time ago an article appeared in *Le Soir* in which Maurice Henrotin says that in the past all breeders believed that pigeons had to be large and strong, because only this type was thought to have enough room for powerful lungs and a strong heart. Breeders felt that the birds had to have mighty muscles, which could only be supported by a sizeable skeleton. This opinion was current until Guillaume Stassart came along with his small and medium-sized light checks, in which the cock very

The pigeon

often looked no different from the hen. They trounced the heavy-duty racers, even in long-distance races.

In *Revue Colombophile* No 15/1960, C. Vanderschelden says the same, 'There was a time when large and heavy pigeons were popular because fanciers believed that success in the sport depended on physical strength. They were strengthened in this belief by the fact that these pigeons performed better than the smaller birds with shorter wings. It did not take long, however, for pigeons to be bred here and there that were much lighter but had long wings.'

'Big and strong versus the smaller build,' says Henrotin. 'Strong and heavy versus the lighter, better wing,' says Vanderschelden. The change has come about as a result of mutation and selection.

I can still remember in the twenties when older breeders, anxious to give a young beginner some guidance, drew my attention to the long, broad back wing which spread across the whole of the back as far as the tail. This is what fanciers wanted, in those days.

A fellow fancier, who also happened to be a very obliging neighbour, showed me with an air of mystery one of his best racers and pointed out a step of about $\frac{5}{8}$ inch between the primaries and secondaries. In those days this was a rarity.

And nowadays? Nearly all pigeons, at least all that are fast over all distances, possess a back wing of medium length and width. This means that the first primary is usually longer than the secondaries (the back wing). The reason for this, I think, is not that the first primary has gradually increased in length but that the back wing is no longer as 'good looking' as it used to be in the past. It is now shorter, and this results in the 'step', which Belgian fanciers call *décalage*.

Since we are talking of primaries, which of today's outstanding racers still have wings with bayonet tips, that is with sharply tapering primaries? Do not all flights now have rounded tips? Once again, this is a case of evolution.

Why have we taken to breeding pigeons with rounded flight

The pigeon

tips? In the beginning we did it unknowingly. Later, when we had the necessary experience, we did it deliberately, because round tips were found to give better performance.

If only breeders would rely a little more on experience instead of listening to foolish tales that are told and retold with not the slightest foundation in fact! Experience is the sum total of knowledge collected in practice, by racing and handling the birds. It also includes the comparison of champion racers aimed at finding both their differences and the most outstanding features they have in common and the dud racers do not have.

What, then, does the typical champion look like? I assume that this is what everybody has been waiting for. In outward appearance, there are different types of champion, no single 'typical' one. A champion is not tied to one particular type. If you look for the crack flyer among the birds in an outstanding loft you will often find that it is the bird which looks most unlike the majority of its loft-fellows. For the champion is an exception in more than one respect, and that frequently includes its appearance.

But if we look for conformity of physical qualities in cracks from all lofts we nearly always find certain features and characteristics which they have in common, although they may be less marked in one than another. We can say therefore that all champions are of one type as far as quality is concerned.

Let us go back to outward appearance. The number of large pigeons is steadily decreasing, that of small pigeons increasing. The general trend is towards the medium-sized pigeon, and it seems to me, on the basis of my own and others' experience, that this is the type that will become more and more popular in the future. Whether large, medium or small, racing over short or long distances, most pigeons these days are slim-built. There may be some short, cobby ones among the champions, but their numbers have declined noticeably and they are only found occasionally among the short-distance racers.

What about deep-keeled, duck-keeled and round? Before I go on I must point out that these expressions, although they are

The pigeon

used by everybody and generally accepted, are not used to mean the same thing by all fanciers. Interpretations of 'duck-keeled' do not differ widely perhaps, but the other two terms mean different things to breeders. Deep-keeled is usually taken to mean V-bottomed, i.e. too deep, and that is undesirable.

I still think that an egg-shaped frame is the ideal shape. It is neither shallow nor deep, but precisely what I mean by 'round'. Take an ordinary hen's egg, hard-boil it and cut it in half lengthwise, from the blunt end towards the pointed one. Scoop out the contents and you are left with an empty half-shell which represents exactly my idea of the ideal shape of a pigeon's underbody.

The run of the sternum may be a little low, but the shell is certainly not V-shaped; it is round. The lowest point is approximately one-third of the way from the blunt end. It does not matter if the pigeon is a little rounder or a little deeper, as long as it is within the golden mean. Remember that you cannot cross a deep-keeled pigeon with a duck-keeled one (i.e. two imperfect birds) in the hope of getting round offspring. The correct way to arrive at the type you want is to mate perfect to imperfect and then weed out, for you will hardly ever succeed at the first attempt.

Not all breeders like round pigeons. In the United States they prefer duck-keeled ones and so apparently do the Germans. In *Flugsport mit Reisetauben* (*The Sport of Pigeon Racing*), Dr. Dorn says that his compatriot Franz Bonfigt aimed at a somewhat compressed shape to the breast.

However, Franz Bonfigt was converted to Louis Vermeijen's view when he visited him once at St. Mariaburg.

A German breeder who visited the loft of Jef Oomens at Breda summed up his opinion of Jef (who is not just any old breeder, let me tell you) in the following words: 'Contrary to German fanciers, he thinks that pigeons with a slightly compressed breastbone are more suitable for the middle-distances. For the long distances he insists on a breastbone which is longer and deeper than that favoured by German breeders. The breast is

The pigeon

not "packed" with muscles. Instead, the muscles lie like small rubber worms alongside the breastbone.'

Huyskens-Van Riel pigeons are not compressed in the breast. They are rounded, but there is a slight, almost imperceptible curve in their sternum. They are a bit fuller than the half egg-shell. But we don't want to be narrow-minded, not when it comes to pigeons of all things. The main thing is that they race well.

If we remember that everything revolves round the question of balance we cannot go far wrong. Balance is commonly defined as a state of rest in which no force exceeds the other. In the case of a pigeon, it means that it is physically and mentally sound. If your pigeon is 'balanced' you can expect it to get into form. I am not saying that it is then automatically in form, but that a fancier who knows his job can get it there.

For outward appearance, which is what we are talking about, 'balance' has another meaning; it means harmony of build, correct proportion of shape in relation to weight. In case any critics are tempted to laugh, I am *not* suggesting that we should go round with scales and tape-measure.

Whenever I have visited famous lofts I have always made a point of asking their owners what they mean by balance, and I have always been told that balance is the indispensable attribute of a good pigeon. In Flanders and Antwerp they tell you it means 'the right proportions'; in the French-speaking provinces they say *'Bien proportionné, il faut de l'harmonie dans la structure'* (well-proportioned, a harmonious structure). Fanciers talk not so much of weight as of the proportion between the wings and the rest of the body.

Whenever I asked how balance was judged the answer was always the same, 'It's difficult to express in words. You have to assess it by eye, holding the bird in your hand and drawing on experience. Surely you have seen and handled enough cracks to have decided what balance looks like in a pigeon?'

So this is how we learn it, by handling champion pigeons. Even if there are exceptions, the rule still holds good.

The pigeon

The breastbone must not have a sharp edge, like a knife, but rather be rounded, like a thin pencil. There must not be much of a gap between the breastbone and the vent bones. In this way we get a bird made in one piece. The vent bones must resist slight pressure without moving back and forward, and they must lie close together.

All fanciers value pigeons with a strong back and rump. If a six-week old youngster has a weak back and rump I get rid of it without any more ado. If a pigeon lacks anything when it is a youngster, it will never acquire it as it grows up, though it can easily lose what it has through the breeder's fault.

Let a pigeon rest in your hand with its head towards you. Push aside the wings with your thumbs, laying bare the back. In nine out of ten cases the pigeon with a weak back and rump will cock up its tail. Pigeons with strong backs sometimes hold their tails horizontally, but more often than not they press the back up and the tail down.

The rump, that is the part between back and tail, must be like a cushion thickly feathered and well padded, and hide most of the tail feathers.

If a youngster has a less powerful back than its parents, decline has set in. The loft is going downhill fast. The truth is often obscured by the fact that in many cases the youngsters still fly very well, although this is usually only the case over short distances and on easy races.

The muscles on either side of the breastbone must feel supple and spring back when lightly pressed. The muscles of older birds, at rest, may feel slightly slack. When a bird is in form, they are tense without feeling hard.

Many racing pigeon journalists do not differentiate between firm and hard, but hard muscles are no good. Hard muscles are like 'a board on either side of the breastbone', Louis Vermeijen used to say. At best they will make a good short-distance racer. Middle and long-distance birds must have supple muscles. The degree of suppleness tells an experienced classifier if a bird is suited for middle or long distances.

The pigeon

If a pigeon has supple muscles they will not feel hard when the bird is in form and its body tense. They will feel firm, because of the tension, but they have lost nothing of their suppleness. No one can judge the quality of supple muscles by casually holding a bird in his hand just once. Muscles can be in various states of tension. They feel different depending on the condition of the pigeon, tired, relaxed, at rest, in form.

Even the expert never classifies the muscles of a pigeon which is not fully grown. Classification cannot be done until the bird is a yearling. The muscles of a youngster, even after the moult, can do no more than give a clue to a promising future.

With a lot of practice, handling many different birds and handling the same birds at different times, you gradually learn to classify by touch alone. You can then say, 'This is only suitable for short distances; this one will go the long-distance limit; that one will be good on difficult long-distance races.'

A strong back, supple muscles and a 'model' wing are three of the most important factors (among many others) that make a pigeon a crack over any distance.

Now let me say something about the wing.

Somville and Vanderschelden must be given the credit for having been the first to do research into the wing and its peculiarities and for having done it with great thoroughness and dedication, for Vanderschelden was no longer young. In his last booklet *Le vade-mecum du Colombiculteur* (*Handbook for Pigeon Fanciers*) Vanderschelden quotes a number of breeders in Belgium and overseas who follow his theory enthusiastically. He say of me: 'Jan Aerts of *De Duif* follows me hesitantly.'

His wing theory has not got through to the large majority of fanciers, as it deserves to. Too many have heard of it but don't pass it on. I deplore this.

Vanderschelden was partly to blame himself. He expected people to agree with him one hundred per cent. Anyone who did not accept his theory without reservation, anyone who contradicted him, ran the risk of incurring his wrath, and he certainly did not mince his words in slaying his opponents. The result

The pigeon

was that many got tired of arguing; they lost interest and stuck to their own opinions.

I do not agree with the standard measurements laid down by his theory and I reject a classification which is based solely on the wing. Does Vanderschelden classify by the wing alone? He is reputed to. Vanderschelden and his followers made the mistake of claiming, true to their theory, that they classified exclusively by the wing. Then they refused to say any more. The only thing they were interested in was the wing; the remainder of the pigeon just did not exist. If any of us pointed out that the pigeon was, after all, a complete entity and did not consist of wings alone, if anybody said that 'there is no single characteristic or quality which controls a pigeon's racing ability', we were shouted down as though we were idiots, talking nonsense.

I do not follow Vanderschelden hesitantly. I go my own way and give the exponent of the wing theory the credit due to him.

I like a pigeon to have feathers like velvet, so that it glides through your hand, and for them to have a soft shine. To me, this pigeon has good feathering.

In judging feathering, we can only be guided by intuition. It is a delicate problem and requires long and frequent practice. Fortunately we have eyes, too, to notice that a pigeon with good feathering also had particularly pliable quills. The power of the wing beat depends on the elasticity of the quill and on the barbs in the web of the feather. Birds with smooth, pliable feathers and quills fly easily and achieve maximum efficiency from minimum effort.

Is there a criterion for classifying flights? There is. If the wing is fanned slowly so that the tips of the feathers glide on top of each other, each tip should bend slightly backwards as though it was reluctant to detach itself from the next feather.

This is proof that the quill in the feather tip is as thin as a hair and bends like one. A feather with this kind of quill isn't in the least like the stalk of a reed. Even the thickest, the innermost

The pigeon

part of the quill, is realitively thin and flexible.

Another indication of flexible quills is when tops of the last four flights curve backwards like the ends of a bow when the bird is at rest. Here is another way of testing the quality of the flight feathers; put several pigeons into a basket so that they are crowded together and leave them for a quarter of an hour or so. When you take the birds out you will notice that those with flexible flight feathers hardly show any signs of having been crowded together; the others will have their flights bent inwards for quite some time afterwards.

A good wing must have a short, well-curved upper arm. The back wing should be straight (none of the feather tips should project when the wing is fanned) and of medium width and length. The first of the primaries is longer than the last of the secondaries adjoining it. The step can be as much as $\frac{3}{4}$ inch. The quills of the first six primaries (counting from the inside) are straight and the tips of the feathers square. They lie in a straight line when the wing is fanned. If the seventh primary projects slightly this is all to the good. The last three feathers are of equal length; sometimes the ninth primary is a little longer than the eighth and tenth. They are slim and have rounded tips and the web along the leading edge narrows to a minimum. The quills of the last primaries bend slightly inwards. When the last four primaries are fanned out the tips must have gaps between them 'large enough to throw peas through'. These are the 'ventilation gaps', which lend power to the wing beat.

I would like to say a special word about the seventh primary. In my opinion it is the most critical feather, the one which accentuates the attributes or faults of the other nine. What conditions must the seventh flight fulfil? Its quill must be as straight as possible. The wider half of the web (the one forming the trailing edge) must be equally wide over almost the entire length of the feather and narrow as close to the tip as possible. The tip must look like the point of a well-worn table knife. The tip of this feather must curve slightly backwards like the end of a bow.

The pigeon

If a pigeon starts to show signs of wear, this can be detected in the seventh primary before anything else. Its quill becomes thicker and feels drier and it has lost its flexibility. It is no longer straight, but curved slightly inwards. That pigeon has had its day. Eyes and muscles, too, provide clues to whether a pigeon is wearing well or wearing out, but nothing is a clearer or earlier sign than the seventh primary. This is why I have made a point of mentioning the seventh primary, as I have done in the past in my lectures and articles.

Feathers with a web of impeccable quality will hardly ever be undulating. Dampness and rain will not harm good feathering. It will dry out quickly after a bath.

The quality of feathering can be judged in a young bird when it is no older than six weeks, but nothing final can be said about the wing until the bird has its third wing. The first is its nest-wing, the second the young-bird wing after the moult, the third the yearling wing after the moult.

I admit that we can learn something from Somville and Vanderschelden, but I refuse categorically to over-emphasize one quality and underestimate all others.

Can we say that there is an ideal type of eye in a pigeon? Which is better—a vertical or a horizontal eye? Just what value has eye-sign? To be honest, I do not even know for sure what eye-sign is. I have read somewhere that it is a little yellow flame in the iris, and elsewhere that it is a circle inside the iris. I have also been told that it is the grey, black or green rim which encircles the iris. I have never bothered to solve the problem, and when I have read what people have to say about the eye-sign, I have thought it not worthwhile to discover the truth, for the writers are far from agreeing on what it is all about and what it is good for.

In my library I have a small pamphlet, *The Use of Eyesigns in Breeding and Racing* by R. C. Silson, which expounds the theory of eye-sign. Either a pigeon has it or it doesn't, it says. It must have it in order to be any good. I quote: 'The real meaning of

The pigeon

eye-sign, what it is and how it works, is still not fully known, but a few current ideas may not be amiss at this point. Firstly, good eye-sign seems to indicate good eyesight. How that eyesight is especially good we don't really know, but somehow it helps birds to home better...' And so it goes on. Nobody really knows what it is and what it is good for, but, in any case, it must be good for something.

Silson goes on, 'Many of the critics have never seen it. They often don't know what to look for and don't want to see it.'

Well, if nobody knows whether the eye-sign is good for anything or not, if nobody knows its real significance, if it only *seems* to indicate good eyesight, then I am one of those critics who have never seen it and who neither need nor want to see it. Let those breeders who have the time and inclination work it out among themselves. When they have reached agreement and can produce facts to prove their theories I shall be only too pleased to listen and be converted.

I am all for an eye with a small pupil, small and lively. If youngsters have larger pupils than their parents things have started to go wrong. Like a weaker back in youngsters, it is one of the first signs of imminent decline.

I like to see a complete ring round the pupil. I prefer this to a partial ring or no ring at all, but if one of my pigeons which does not have a ring wins top prizes and regularly beats another pigeon which has one, then I gladly part with the latter. As far as the youngsters bred from either bird are concerned I stick to the principle of judging the tree by its fruit.

I never argue about colour, on principle. I like a one-colour eye, a so-called bull eye, as much as I like a two-colour eye, as long as the colour is bright and clear and the eye shiny and dry. In both cases, however, the colour of the iris must darken towards its outer edge. An eye which is pale, dull and lifeless, that looks as if it were covered with a veil, points to decline, old-age or illness.

I am also in favour of an eye which is nicely enclosed by the

The pigeon

eyelids, so that little or none of the eyeball is visible beyond the iris. I also prefer an eye in which the pupil is slightly biased towards the beak. Why? I have found this in many good pigeons but rarely or never in poorer ones.

I think there is something in the 'star eye', i.e. an eye which has very fine lines radiating outwards through the iris. Very often these are hardly visible to the naked eye, but they become increasingly obvious when the pigeon is in form. I like the star eye because it is a sign of improving form. It can usually be seen in good racers.

I like an iris which is bordered by a thin rim. Some call this the eye-sign. In winter the rim is grey. With improving form it changes from dark grey to black or blackish-green. Like the darkening of the outer edges of the iris itself, this is a sign of form. It is caused by an increased flow of blood to the brain.

I like a lively eye because, together with the pigeon's whole appearance and behaviour, it gives me a clue to the bird's condition.

Anything we can detect in a pigeon with our five senses helps us to learn something about it. We recognize a champ and a dud and form an opinion, however limited, about each bird.

But we remain forever ignorant of what a pigeon really has in it. What about the heart and lungs, the air-sacks and the digestive organs? Are we looking at a bird with an economical metabolism or is there much wastage? At what temperature does it perform best? We can only guess.

Then there is the bird's character and intelligence (breeders' language!). We know nothing about these. The basket provides us with the answers to all questions we cannot solve with our five senses, in other words, the 'spiritual' world of our pigeons.

Will we ever know any more? Perhaps. But at the moment we are still forced to ask, 'What do we know of a pigeon?' It is an enigma, a question-mark on wings. In a way this is fortunate. If it were different, where would the excitement be in our sport? If the great secret were known, the enchantment might be gone forever.

9

Back from the race

A recurring complaint, heard every season, is, 'At first my pigeons raced quite well, then they gradually fell off and about half-way through the season they could hardly win a tail prize.'

This always sparks off a discussion. One argument invites another, which is a very good thing, for argument is at the heart of science.

My own contribution to it is summed up in this quotation: 'The constant pressure of work in mechanized and cost-productive industries, and the attendant worries; the press, radio and television with their alarming reports on politics and catastrophies; the continual dissemination of the "latest news" which at one time scarcely reached the masses; all these stresses, without sufficient opportunity to relax, overtax our nerves. Our bodies suffer from an accumulation of waste products and the cells can only be cleansed by rest.' This applies just as much to pigeons as it does to people, and I say this in all seriousness.

We know that all pigeons carry protozoa in their crops. Normally harmless, they lie in wait for some weakening of the body to produce the dreaded canker. If I maintain that the cells of any organism, be it human or pigeon, can only be cleansed by rest, many people will contradict me. They will point out that recent research has shown cortisone and aspartic acid to be effective cleansers.

My counter-argument is that fatigue in human beings as well

Back from the race

as pigeons is hardly ever confined to physical fatigue alone. The muscles may be tired, true, but more dangerous than this muscular tiredness is the mental tiredness brought about by nervous stress. Let us take a look at both.

I think I am right in saying that ninety per cent of our fanciers have only small lofts containing a limited number of pigeons. Anyone who has two or three outstanding racers is a local champion. It takes strong self-restraint to handle the 'luxury' of wealth. The man who has a champion in his loft is constantly tempted to race the bird week after week and demand much more of it than is justifiable. The same is true of those bigger breeders who do not stop at middle-distance races, but go on to the difficult long-distance races to compete with the élite of their home country and often other countries too.

In the lofts of both small and big breeders the crack bird is the exception, and it is on this prodigy that the heaviest burden is imposed.

While the small breeder races his crack every week without a break, the big breeder races his long-distance birds five or six times a season, even though common sense should tell him that four times, or even three times if one race is a particularly difficult one, would be more than enough. In this way the best pigeons are over-worked because they are not given enough rest, then their owners come along and complain of tired pigeons without stamina. There may be another side to it; the birds may be physically tired, or they may be tired of trying.

This condition is mainly found in short and middle-distance racers. The birds are exercised for an hour both morning and evening every day and can hardly be expected to suffer from physical exhaustion. These birds are normally raced in an over-excited state because their owners exploit jealousy and fighting for the nest box and nest bowl (I am talking here only of races that take the birds away from the loft for one single night).

We have a system in Belgium by which short-distance birds are raced from a 'single-box loft'. This is playing with fire. Each cock lives with his hen in a separate small loft in which there is

Back from the race

only one nest box. Before the cock is sent on a race a 'stranger' is put in with the hen. After a nerve-racking fight with the strange cock and with the memory of it foremost in his mind, the cock is put into the basket. Widower birds see their hens too often and for too long before they are basketed. Small wonder that their nerves are strained to the limit.

Then the fancier complains of his pigeons dropping off form half-way through the season! He wonders what the cause might be and comes to the fatal conclusion that they are overtired and listless because they are tired of racing, and he continues with his wrong system. But the pigeons are no longer game. They are tired of being driven.

The breeder has only himself to blame. Unless he wants to spoil his birds permanently for racing he must call a temporary halt and let the birds have a rest.

Whenever anybody asks for my advice, my reply is always the same, 'You've had it for this season. Give the cock his hen and let him lead a normal life; drive, hatch and feed their young, and repeat the same cycle all over again. And let it be a lesson to you for next season!'

My advice is hardly ever followed and if it is I hear later that the fancier has subsequently concentrated all his attention on young-bird racing. The evil has been shifted but not banished. The young birds, which should only be exercised and trained, since they are, after all, still growing, are now asked to do much more than their fair share. So now the young birds are exhausted and possibly spoilt for the future. They may still be quite satisfactory as yearlings—perhaps!—but the vicious circle has started all over again. The late Dr. J. C. Bom, who was as well-known in Holland as a pigeon fancier as he was as a physician, wrote in *The Rational Feeding of Racing Pigeons*:

'It has been calculated from practical experience that the maximum distance the majority of pigeons should be raced, looked at from the point of view of sportsmanship, lies around 300 miles. After this a pigeon loaded with glycogen has used up its reserves and is drawing on body protein. The 300 miles must

Back from the race

be covered at a speed which means the bird being on the wing for ten to eleven hours at the outside.'

Let us examine this train of thought a little more closely. What Dr. Bom has to say is worth listening to. He did extremely well in the difficult races from Pau, Dax and Barcelona. He was a great man, not only as a physician.

He is talking about 'the majority of pigeons', which does not include the champs, the aces, for they are exceptions. The upper limit of 300 miles in ten to eleven hours does not apply to them. If we work out the velocity for Dr. Bom's figures we find that it is very low, about 880 yards per minute. In Belgium we associate this kind of snail's pace with an abnormally difficult, rotten race. But let's leave the low velocity as it is. I daresay 300 miles at 880 yards per minute are more difficult than 450 miles at 1320 yards per minute (ten hours in either case), and 450 miles falls into the long-distance category.

A velocity of 1320 over a long distance is what we call 'pigeon weather' here. It is the kind of weather that makes the pigeons work. A true fancier is certainly not keen on 880 because it means a far too difficult race. On the other hand, he would not want a tail wind to carry the birds home. They have to work, he says. As long as they do that he is satisfied, because then he can sift the wheat from the chaff.

Most of our long-distance races exceed 450 miles. If we are to believe Dr. Bom then all our birds will have spent their reserves and started to draw on their body protein by the time they reach home. On a longer and more difficult race (for instance from Marseille, with its fierce mistral) there is even the danger that muscle tissue will be called upon.

Most fanciers believe that a pigeon replaces burnt-up muscle tissues very quickly, but this recovery is purely superficial. We cannot measure how much the muscles have suffered.

Quite often a pigeon regains its unruffled feathering after just a few hours and the fancier is fooled into thinking that it has fully recovered. If he must go by superficial appearance he would do better to ignore the feathering and look at the nostrils

Back from the race

and the eyes, especially the eyes—they have lost colour. Even if the bird has not had to battle against rain or a headwind, watch the eyes. The iris is bound to have lost some colour on the first day, however little. There is less sparkle in the eye. You can see the difference if you put your champion next to a bird that has stayed at home and compare the two. It is the small things you have to look for, the seemingly insignificant ones, for they can tell you a great deal, if only you know how to interpret them. If the bird feels plump and round a short time after it has returned from a race, or even on the following day, there can be no question of complete recovery.

Any fancier who is sensitive to these things can tell for quite some time afterwards that the muscles have not yet regained their former tension. Another infallible sign is the pigeon's weight. Before it has fully recovered, it must have regained its former weight, and it will certainly not have done so during the first few days.

The used-up muscle tissue must be replaced, and so the body must first of all be cleansed of the waste products that have accumulated as a result of the burning of body protein. As long as the blood is not purified of waste products it cannot build up new reserves.

We must give the pigeon the necessary rest and also help nature in its task, but not by using laxatives as is a habit with some fanciers, nor with products which unbalance the organism directly or indirectly by straining the heart, kidneys or liver.

We can, of course, resort to mineral salts and vegetable extracts, but they are only effective if they are given in small doses and for several days. Don't, under any circumstances, administer large doses of anything. Purging is nearly always harmful to the birds, particularly in the middle of the racing season. Some people are in favour of honey, glucose and dextrose, even small quantities of cortisone and aspartic acid. As for me, I remain true to my principle, 'Nothing but food and water'. I am against any 'doses'.

I advise complete rest (even for those pigeons which do not

Back from the race

return exhausted), screening-off excessive daylight and a light diet consisting mainly of summer barley.

When a bird comes home it should find fresh drinking water, at loft temperature, and a small quantity of light food to satisfy its sharpest hunger. When it has recovered a little from the effort of the race, it should be allowed to fill its crop with light food.

Many Belgian breeders feed only barley after a race. Others mix it with maize, dari, wheat, rice and breadcrumbs. I have nothing against the mixture, as long as the food is natural and does not burden the digestive organs.

Regardless of how difficult Sunday's race was, Monday is always a light-diet day. The change-over to the richer diet depends on how great the effort was and when and how far the next race is.

After the exertions of a race the pigeons will need a period of rest, especially if it was a particularly hard race. If their next race is also to be a difficult one it is advisable to let the birds stay at home for one Sunday; in which case they do not go back on to their normal, heavier diet until the Friday before the Sunday off. The pigeons must not be in top form while they are resting. Top condition must not be induced until the end of the second week, i.e. shortly before they are sent off on another race.

I believe many fanciers act differently. 'The pigeons have worked hard,' they say, 'fine. Let's strike while the iron is hot.' And they don't let them have a week's rest. But if the birds are completely rested they are certain to add a few yards per minute to their velocities on the next race. This is the attitude most sensible and capable fanciers take. Competition in Belgium, which is rightly called the cradle of pigeon racing, is extremely keen and the stakes are usually very high. It is, therefore, not surprising that fanciers resort to every available means to beat the opposition.

Not infrequently, fanciers go to the lengths of doping their pigeons or, at least, giving them extra doses of vitamins. The high stakes involved make people lose their common sense, but

Back from the race

experience and statistics reveal the truth; it is only by rest and complete recovery from previous efforts that pigeons maintain a consistent performance throughout the season. All other aids only lead to temporary success, and even then it is questionable whether they have the desired effect.

Anything against the pigeon's nature ruins a loft.

As I have said before, nobody can judge how much or how little a bird's muscle tissue has suffered during a race. We can feel and see that it has suffered, but our observations are only superficial and cannot be relied on. We can only guess the extent of the damage done, but it is important that we should know when the muscle tissue is completely restored. To find this out, we have to watch our pigeons during their daily exercise round the loft. We can make judgements about a bird's feathering, weight, the suppleness and tension of its muscles, the colour of its iris; but the most important clue is the bird's behaviour on the wing.

After a difficult race the birds are not usually very interested in flying much or for long periods. If the weather is cold and rainy, it is better to keep them in the loft. On the Monday following a race they usually fly low round the loft. They don't go far and soon come back. They know for themselves that they ought to take it easy. It is a sign of complete recovery when they fly off high and fast in a flock and stay away for several minutes. When they return they behave as though they did not know the loft and fly straight past it and off in another direction. This can go on for quite some time, an hour or longer. From time to time they make a rush for the roof or actually sit down, but only through playfulness. They take off again and repeat the same manoeuvre until, at last, with drooping heads and flapping wings, they circle a few times round the loft and pitch. Once they behave in this way we know for sure that they have fully recovered and no trace of fatigue is left. However, there is one reservation.

Pigeons always like to fly in flocks. While most of the flock has fully recovered there may be some individuals in it which do not stay in the air for so long. They probably don't feel like

Back from the race

flying at all, but they are being carried along by the mob. These birds had better stay in the loft. We must keep an eye on them, because they are obviously not as strong as the others. We should make a note of this; it will come in useful later.

If, on the other hand, all the pigeons have stayed together in the flock, if none of them have gone off by themselves or come back before the others, we can congratulate ourselves. These are the birds that will be out in front next race day, and we can confidently put another shilling on them. They are in top form; they don't know what to do with their abounding energy.

How many fanciers are there who know this? And how many of those who do can wait for the birds to show this behaviour before they get them keyed up for racing? Not many! I speak from experience, years of experience with the best breeders in the country. It is only the man who gives his attention to these points who can be said to practice pigeon racing at an advanced level.

Out of a number of different approaches, the one that is backed by objectivity and sober reason is the most reliable. This is the approach of the master breeders and we should take a leaf out of their book.

The same rules apply to birds raced on the natural system. They are busy and restless. They fly constantly back and forward, enter the loft and take off again. They do not fly as high, as far or as long as the widower birds. They show their vitality by gliding and flapping their wings.

While the behaviour of widower birds scarcely differs from one individual to another, birds raced on the natural system need close individual observation.

Some indicate top form by ceaselessly collecting nesting material, either brought in from the fields or stolen from another box in the loft. They are intensely busy building their nests, which often take on quite sizeable proportions. Others cannot bear another pigeon anywhere near their nest box. If they are in low form or not completely recovered they are quite indifferent.

Racing pigeons on the natural system requires more skill and

Back from the race

is more interesting than racing on widowerhood. It is certainly more instructive. This is why I would advise all beginners to race on the natural system first, before taking up widowerhood. I am not revealing any secrets in saying that good breeders never race yearlings on widowerhood. There is more than one reason for this.

Yearlings with two young birds in the nest should only lose a very little weight. If they do not pass this test they have to go, as I pointed out when talking about Matterne's loft at Overhespen. They must be able to go through the usual, natural cycle of driving, hatching, feeding their young, without any trouble. It is a normal process which cannot harm their development if they are healthy birds. The nest will also tie them more closely to the loft and their mate, and this will have a beneficial influence on their racing performance.

Pigeons raced on the natural system cannot be raced with equal success every week, not because of the distance, but because the birds are not in form every week. With pigeons raced on the natural system, form comes and goes according to the phases of the breeding cycle. So why race them against other birds that are in top form? It would only be a waste of money.

So the yearlings are trained but not raced hard. It is more a case of revising and improving on what they have learnt as young birds.

Last, but not least, there is the advantage that on the natural system the yearling hens can be raced, too; that is, those among them that have proved outstanding as youngsters. While one of a pair is away on a race, the other can rest. This avoids the danger of over-working them. Racing yearling hens, and older ones too, establishes their value as racers and is a useful guide to selecting breeding stock.

In the Antwerp Union hens are raced on the difficult middle-distances and long-distances, either competing against each other or duplicated with widower birds. They are frequently successful. More and more hens are raced over long distances if

Back from the race

liberation takes place so late in the day that the birds cannot reach home the same day but have to 'camp out' for the night. The fancier here relies on maternal instinct. Hens go to sleep later at night and get up earlier in the morning than cocks. Did you know that? The Dutch know it and so do the British, because in these countries overnight races are won as frequently by hens as they are by cocks. In Belgium hens are not raced very much. I think this is a pity. I shall never cease to encourage fanciers whenever I can to give good hens a chance to make use of their talents in racing.

I should like to say a few words now on why I find the natural system more interesting than widowerhood.

First let me explain what I mean by interesting. I mean that you can learn more from the natural system; it offers a better opportunity of discovering the nature of a pigeon. You come to realize that all pigeons are different, not necessarily in build, feathering or even performance, but in 'character', in 'intelligence' using these words in the sense the pigeon fancier attaches to them—to know that all pigeons are individualists. Quite by the way you also learn to be a better breeder.

You can learn more and you can learn it better by this system if you take the trouble, even if you are a slow learner.

No matter how able we might become as breeders, we will always find masters with something to teach us. There will always be breeders who are better than anybody else, who know more and perform better, simply because they are more talented. For there is no doubt that in all fields of activity, whether pigeon racing, working with pick and shovel, pen-pushing or driving a donkey, there are people who have more aptitude than the others. In every profession, in every trade, we find master craftsmen, capable workers and botchers.

I once told a fancier that I thought pigeons were individualists and asked him whether he agreed. He said 'Yes', but he really meant egoists. Well, there are plenty of those, among people as well as animals. As far as pigeons are concerned, I mean that no two pigeons are alike, that each pigeon differs from all others of

Back from the race

its species, however little. How it differs can only be discovered by each man in his own loft, and this takes more than just a little skill.

I know that people are addicted to fishing (my eldest son, who has no interest whatever in pigeons, is one of them), but if I had to go fishing I would take a book and a sheet of paper along, and before long I would be so absorbed in my book that the fish could help themselves to my bait.

When I go into a pigeon loft I don't need to take a book with me. There is too much to see and learn. This is why I cannot understand why so few fanciers can bear to spend an hour among their pigeons without talking or doing something.

The whole of the loft is a stage. The performance is real, presented by actors who know their parts. To them it is not an act, of course, for animals do not make believe.

You will profit from your observations in the loft when you come to send the birds off to races. You now know how to handle and feed them to prepare them for racing. If they have been keyed up in this way they will not waste your money if they are at all capable of winning. If they are not, then you will know that you have got out of them all there is in them, and that they are simply not up to standard. You can dispatch them without regret, for there is no ace among them.

Suppose one of your cocks wins a top prize. Nobody would have expected it, but you think you know the reason, for the day after he was basketed his hen laid an egg. The cock knew, but you didn't. You could have known, however. The cock would have told you in his own way. You could have seen from the change in his behaviour that he was in peak form, but he couldn't tell you because you weren't there. You have learned another lesson. Now you know that widower cocks fly just that bit faster if their hens are about to lay.

If you find an egg somewhere in the loft of the widow hens, you must make every effort to discover which of the hens has 'lost' the egg, for her cock cannot be trusted the following Sunday. The week before, you could have pooled him, because

Back from the race

his hen was about to lay, but now he knows that it was a 'false alarm' and has lost interest.

When I explain something like this to fanciers in my area they nod understandingly. They have got the point. It is these small, apparently insignificant things which distinguish the successful fancier from all the others.

Here is another example. You have all your young birds together in one loft. After a few training tosses you want to send them off on their first race. You would dearly like to know what they are capable of, but only the clock will be able to tell you for sure. You have put your hopes on one young cock in particular. You know his pedigree and you have confidence in him. He is a bird very much to your liking, so you risk a pool. What happens? He is not first home; another cock is clocked in several minutes before him.

The same thing happened to me quite often many years ago. Today I would no longer be taken in, for during the week preceding the race the cock who eventually came first paraded across the loft floor like a soldier. Head held high, he made movements with his beak and tongue as though he had tasted something delicious. I did not understand his behaviour. During the following week, I noticed this strange behaviour in a number of other young cocks. They had become mature. The following week's winner was the first to reach maturity and look across his shoulder at the young hens.

As soon as you notice this behaviour among the cocks, you must separate them from the hens in the following week. Before they are basketed, put a few old cocks in with the young hens and a few old hens with the young cocks. The young birds are not given the opportunity to mate, but they have been roused and they will come storming home. This is an excellent system by which young birds often fly better than old birds who have been mated.

Don't ask me which bird to put your money on. Nobody can know the answer to that, least of all someone sitting behind a typewriter. It is something which every fancier must find out for

Back from the race

himself, for he is the one who can watch his birds' behaviour in the loft.

In the first week, it was one among many who gave the signal. Now many are aroused and eager and so excited that you hope they will have a headwind race. If they are liberated in a tail wind they may return in the evening from the wrong direction.

I have picked on a few examples at random, but the number I could cite are legion. For a complete study of the subject every man has to go and watch his own birds.

I would like to add just one point. Pigeons raced on the natural system are less likely to be overtired. Widower cocks can be raced nearly every week, and in this way they are overworked. But pigeons raced on the natural system must be given at least three Sundays off in any five or six, because they are in the wrong position on the nest to be in peak condition. A good fancier never sends off a bird which is not in peak condition.

I have now given you a few hints on winning systems. For very good reasons I have concentrated mainly on the natural system, which gives the birds a natural rest. There is one other thing.

When I was fifteen I spent the summer holiday with my uncle. Since he was a pigeon fancier, I also inspected his loft. I noticed at once the 'clean' smell under the roof tiles. My uncle's loft was always kept clean and could pass muster at any time, but I had not noticed that particular smell before. When I asked, he explained to me that it was an insecticide, a particularly good one against gnats and lice. Pigeons must be able to get a good night's rest without being plagued by parasites. So my uncle said. That was in 1913.

In 1947 I first got to know the Huyskens-Van Riel loft at Ekeren-Donk. Huyskens had climbed on to the roof by a ladder and was busy spraying the gaps between the roof tiles and between the small ventilation tiles. I wanted to know what he was doing. He said, 'Jan old chap, they have to get a good night's sleep without being pestered by gnats.' 1913–1947, an interval of thirty-four years. I had long forgotten the lesson my uncle

Back from the race

had taught me. Well, what do you think of that? For many years Huyskens-Van Riel were winners of all the races far and near.

Isn't a good insecticide a hundred times better than potions from bottles and pills from boxes which shorten the recovery period?

The things we do to make sure our pigeons get some rest and can recover in peace and quiet!

I should mention that Frans Huyskens' brother is a well-known doctor who knows many pharmaceutical products and their properties, but he always advised that pigeons should be kept and raced naturally.

I should say 'as far as advice was necessary', for both Huyskens and Van Riel were too good for me to suggest that they were in need of any advice. They were too objective and unsentimental, both in pigeon racing and their professions.

10

How do our pigeons find their way home?

A few years ago fanciers in Belgium suffered severe losses of young birds off the roof for two seasons running. Bad weather and changeable seasons were partly to blame, but something else played a part. If these had been isolated cases they would not be worth writing about, but the losses were general and unusually heavy. Some fanciers even went so far as to blame sinister forces or atmospheric disturbances.

I refuse to believe any such theory, for there were some lofts which suffered few losses or none at all. If we discount the unfavourable weather conditions we are left with the normal losses that occur in every season.

We are forced therefore to look for the cause within the fanciers themselves. For why should one loft be subject to these unknown forces while a neighbouring loft escapes unscathed?

There are other problems which are a headache to many fanciers.

Why do their birds hardly ever return home from the right direction? Is there anything that can be done to solve this problem? It is all too easy to talk about intelligent or stupid pigeons, about a more or less developed sixth or seventh sense. This brings us to the question of sense of direction and orientation in birds, a subject that I feel ought to be given some space in this book. I shall begin with landmarks and sense of direction.

How do our pigeons find their way home?

There is a world of difference between our lay approach and that of scientists. We are too fond of saying: 'I *suppose* this is the way it works . . .' or 'this *must* be the answer.' But we should not try to get out of it so easily. We ought to approach the question very seriously and try to find an answer about which there can be no doubt.

It is no good being satisfied with the results of a single experiment or one which has been inadequately prepared, because they are accidental and unreliable. A single result is never conclusive; it never even provides reliable clues. Only after a series of experiments can a general rule be drawn up, and then there are often exceptions. Two or three results which are basically the same may show quite dissimilar outward manifestations.

Let us assume that pigeons which sneeze and scratch their heads suffer from worms. Our verdict is coryza, chronic cold. We give the necessary nasal treatment with some proven anit-coryza preparation, but the worms remain. The birds continue to sneeze and scratch their heads.

From this we can conclude that a correct verdict can only be reached after a series of well-prepared experiments. The results must be noted, so that they can be thoroughly analysed. This series of experiments, statistics and analyses will be the basis of a reliable theory, one based on facts.

Let us return to our original problem of heavy losses and see what Dr. Whitney has to say.

Dr. Whitney, who bought his birds from the best-known lofts (he could certainly tell a good bird and never begrudged the price) lost an alarming number of birds, many more than any other fancier in the neighbourhood. I say 'neighbourhood'. In Belgium houses are built on top of each other and there is a pigeon loft every few yards. Where Dr. Whitney lives a fancier who lives miles away is still a 'neighbour'.

Dr. Whitney wanted to know the reasons behind his unusually heavy losses. He told me that he had sixty young birds flying round his loft, which is situated right in the middle of extensive forests. They never ventured out of sight of the loft. When they

How do our pigeons find their way home?

were three to four months old they were sent on two- three- and five-mile training tosses. As they spiralled up into the sky they could easily make out their loft which was in a clearing about 2½ acres in size, amid a sea of green. Sometimes they flew off in the wrong direction but always returned home in the end. Then they were sent on a ten-mile toss. Out of sixty young birds only fourteen returned, and those not even on the same day. To provide himself with enough yearlings for the next season, Dr. Whitney bred more youngsters and also had sixteen youngsters given to him by a friend. Training was continued as far as New York, which lies in a south-westerly direction, so the birds should have returned from the south-west. But they flew in from the south-east. The drag of strange pigeons had carried them home, but not by the most direct route. Three miles to the south-east of the loft there was a high water tower which served as a landmark. The pigeons had followed the irregular coastline with the drag instead of turning off inland. Dr. Whitney's loft is six miles from the coast. Most of the other lofts are on the coast itself.

Your first reaction will be that nothing has been proved. The story only shows that the birds followed the drag too long. They should have broken away sooner. But don't jump to conclusions!

In the first race Dr. Whitney entered fifteen pigeons. He sent another forty-five along for a training toss. They were liberated an hour later. The distance was 100 miles. Thirty-one of the forty-five returned in the following week. Six more returned later still.

The fifteen birds entered in the race returned normally, but they had once again followed the coast and covered an additional nine miles. They had not taken the shortest route because they had not broken away from the drag.

One of Dr. Whitney's friends then advised him not to train his birds on their own but to send them on the training truck along with everyone else's birds. At first all went well. But when the 50-mile stage had been reached—this was a training toss by training truck—he lost forty birds out of sixty-eight. These

How do our pigeons find their way home?

exceptionally heavy losses continued till 1961. None of the other fanciers suffered comparable losses. What could be the reason for his failure?

In 1960 one single bird returned from the west, all on its own. This happened on every training toss. Half a mile west of the loft there stood a windmill. Apparently the pigeon had chosen this for a landmark. When the bird's arrival at the windmill was checked it was discovered through field-glasses to be coming from the direction of two water towers on the top of a hill $3\frac{1}{2}$ miles south-west of the windmill.

From then on the birds were trained along the line of windmill to water towers. Day after day they were liberated two miles behind the towers until they homed from the right direction. This training was mainly for the benefit of the yearlings and old birds.

There can be no doubt that pigeons learn to recognize landmarks in the neighbourhood of their loft and use them as signposts on their way home. Without the windmill and water towers Dr. Whitney's losses would have been even greater, even though his birds were from the best lofts in Belgium, Scotland and England.

This left the problem of the youngsters who did not dare to fly far from the loft, who did not want to explore. Eventually he hit on the idea of erecting his own signpost. He chose a mast 95 feet high, which projected 30 feet above the treetops. On top of it he put a brass sphere, a landmark that could be seen from a distance of three miles with the naked eye.

After it was installed, a written daily record was kept, exact to the minute, of how the young birds reacted to the strange object that had been set up about fifty yards from the loft. It was found that the pigeons gradually went farther and farther away from the loft, and for longer periods, and thus came to know more of the surroundings.

It would take too long to describe the progress of the story in every detail. Suffice to say that success in racing eventually followed. In the following year only two out of forty-two young

How do our pigeons find their way home?

birds were lost in a training toss with a training truck in which 1,800 birds took part. However, the birds still did not return by the most direct route but followed the drag for too long along the coast. But the mast had its effect. The additional distance flown was less and the losses dropped noticeably.

What conclusions can we draw from this story? Young birds seek first of all to explore the surroundings of their loft within a fairly wide radius. Prominent landmarks undoubtedly help them to find their way back to the loft.

According to Dr. Whitney the entire phenomenon of homing includes several distinct divisions:

1. The pigeon possesses an innate behaviour pattern which we call a homing drive.
2. The young birds, once they have reached a certain proficiency in flying, want to explore the neighbourhood to learn the landmarks, but they will not go off to explore unless there is some point of recognition close to home.
3. After many exploratory flights, after they have become acquainted with suitable landmarks and points of recognition near the loft, and after many training tosses during which the birds learn what to expect on races, returning home on the shortest possible route becomes a habit.
4. To return home from distant race points, pigeons, like all migratory birds, use the sun compass. On the last part of the way they use familiar landmarks as guides.

Although circumstances differ from case to case, all fanciers are faced with more or less the same problems. For Dr. Whitney the problem was a small clearing in the middle of extensive forests without a single other pigeon loft nearby. In our country there is no shortage of landmarks. But every day pigeons are out on training tosses organized by smaller or larger clubs. They rush across the countryside carrying the young birds along with them and leading them off-course.

Belgium is a densely populated country and wherever you go in the open countryside you are likely to see half a dozen church

How do our pigeons find their way home?

spires on the horizon, not counting other buildings, rivers, streams and canals and all the other landmarks which our pigeons use as signposts to their lofts. And still a large number of young birds are lost and never find their lofts again.

I remember the late Jan Verstraeten, formerly a judge at Puurs. As soon as it was dark the old gentleman used to go up into his attic loft and throw all the windows and traps wide open. He told me that he very rarely lost young birds off the roof because they were out before they could really fly. As soon as the first cock crowed, they were out on the roof greeting the rising sun. Like the fledglings of birds of prey balancing on the edge of their nests, they hopped along the ridge of the roof and the gutters flapping their wings and pretending to fly with their feet never quite leaving the ground. On their first flights round the loft they were taken by the old nesting birds, then they gradually went farther and farther with the birds of neighbouring lofts.

When Verstraeten went up into his loft after breakfast old and young birds were given their first feed. None of them was missing. After two or three weeks, it happened occasionally that some young birds did not turn up for breakfast. As time went on their number increased. But they all reappeared around midday and waited for their lunch. Verstraeten never worried if some of his young birds did not come back for hours. Frequently they did not return until the evening. If they were carried miles away from home by a flock of strange pigeons out on a training toss they could come to no harm because they had previously done their exploring and got to know the countryside within a wide radius of the loft. Very few birds were lost.

Jef Van Riel had to use a different approach because his loft was surrounded by fanciers racing on widowerhood who gave their widowers an open loft for training flights in the surrounding district as soon as it was daylight. These widowers presented a great danger to Jef's young birds. For this reason he did not let his youngsters out on the roof until the afternoon and he kept a watchful eye on them. Only when they were more

How do our pigeons find their way home?

experienced—after a few weeks—did he let them out in the morning. Then he started to train them, and he, too, suffered only very small losses.

Even as I write this, he tells me how surprised he is at the many complaints about heavy losses of young birds. 'Will they never learn?' he says. 'Can't they see that youngsters need to be taught, and that the first 'lessons' are the most important as far as their youth and later life are concerned?'

From all this and from my own experience during a mere half-century I have come to the following conclusion. Of all the senses a pigeon possesses, sight is the most important. Through it, the bird gets to know objects better than through any other sense. Through it, the bird becomes acquainted with its immediate surroundings. It follows that young birds must be given the opportunity, over a fairly long period, to see as many objects as possible, firstly in the immediate vicinity and then within a larger radius, so that they can learn to tell them apart!

The Greek philosopher, Aristotle, taught that there are three degrees of recognition in animals and that in the highest degree, which pigeons possess, the sense of recollection (i.e. memory) plays an essential part.

Something can only become imprinted in the memory, firmly enough never to be forgotten, if it is seen time and time again. The more often we have seen something the more readily we can recognize it by its outward appearance and behaviour. It goes without saying that all our senses must be trained. This is best done while we are young, for what we learn while we are young we retain throughout life. This holds good for animals as well as man.

Your young birds must get to know the surroundings of the loft and the race route. You must give them all the time and opportunity to do just that, always taking the necessary precautionary measures.

When he was looking for a remedy against his heavy losses of young birds, Dr. Whitney found the answer in one single pigeon which came home from the 'right direction', because it had not

How do our pigeons find their way home?

followed the drag along the coast but made for the signpost it had discovered.

This brings me to my second point; why is it that our pigeons often return from a race from the wrong direction? What can we do to overcome this? Has this anything to do with sense of direction?

If you enter your birds outside your own club, say in a race where the majority of birds race home along a route which differs more or less from that your own birds ought to fly, then there is always a danger of your birds following the drag and adding so much to their mileage that they stand little chance of finishing in the lead. It has been found, however, that this nearly always happens if the birds are not in peak form.

I will explain how this comes about.

Some years ago, on a Sunday morning, I followed a race along the Compiègne-Noyon-St. Quentin route in my car. As the birds were liberated at Compiègne (154 miles) they made off in a bunch. Whed the next bunch was liberated I was parked about two miles from Compiègne station to get a view of the birds at a later stage and discovered that the bunch had dissolved into a long front. The pigeons were 'advancing' in one line, except for some slower birds.

A few miles farther on the front line was already broken up. There were several large gaps. Although the majority of birds still formed a wide front there were some spearhead groups which were gradually pulling away.

Any bird which is caught in the drag is beaten. It will continue in the wrong direction. Birds in peak form get out in front and are not bothered in this way. They can easily break away from their opponents and choose the most direct route home. Most of the other pigeons will follow the drag on their way home. A pigeon likes to fly with the flock and it is wise to remember this when calculating the chances of your birds and in deciding on which races to send them. The town or the region which enters the majority of birds in a race obviously has an advantage over odd birds from outlying districts. The advantage decreases, however,

How do our pigeons find their way home?

as the distance increases. Over long distances birds come home singly and run less risk of following the wrong direction.

There are other factors influencing the choice of route home. For example, there is the wind, and the time of liberation, but I shall come back to these later.

To further substantiate what I have just said I would like to tell you of a few personal experiences. Some years ago I had gone out to the Huyskens-Van Riel loft at Ekeren to witness the arrival of their pigeons in the inter-provincial race from Angoulême, organized by the East Flanders Union. The five birds the team had entered were going to have their work cut out against the best lofts in Flanders. It was left to these five to defend the honour of Antwerp.

Suddenly the telephone rang. It was a call from their friends, the Cattrysse brothers from Moere, in West Flanders, who announced that they had just sighted two early birds. Immediately, calculations were made to see how much time the birds had left not to be beaten.

Some were still busy with figures when Jef Van Riel whispered to me, 'Leave them to their arithmetic, it's neither here nor there. They must come in from the oil storage tanks at Hoboken, over the harbour and the dome of the Antwerp main station which you can just see in the distance. If we get one coming in from that direction it will have broken away from the drag and be in the lead. If not, all is lost.'

Jef was right. The first bird came in from over Antwerp main railway station and won the big pool. The other four birds won very nice prizes, too. But they did not come from due south-west as the first bird did. We noticed a slight deviation to the west. The fifth pigeon even came from the polder, from the Scheldt, which is almost due west. The last four birds had obviously stayed longer with the drag of pigeons from Flanders.

The conclusion is that it is mainly the drag which determines the route. Strong fliers, birds that are in peak form, can break away from the drag and are not bothered by it. This is why they come from the right direction. Pigeons can be helped to do this

How do our pigeons find their way home?

by the way they are trained; that is, by the choice of route over which they are trained as youngsters.

Louis Pepermans lives at Zemst, a small village in Brabant. The large fraternity of Brussels fanciers allows all those fanciers who live within a radius of nine miles of the Brussels town hall to compete in their races. If a single fancier in a village lives within this radius all the fanciers in that village may enter the races. Zemst is an exception. Zemst fanciers may only race with Brussels fanciers in the provincial races of the Brabant Union, which are middle and long-distance races, but I will not go into the reasons for this here.

So every Sunday, Pepermans has to look round for a different club to race with. This frequently means he has to go to Lier, a small town 15 miles north-east of Zemst as the crow flies. You do not have to be a Belgian fancier to know that the loft which has a smaller distance measurement *and* lies outside the main line of flight will be beaten in nine out of ten cases. For this reason, only Lier fanciers and those from outlying villages that have a greater distance measurement race in the Lier club. For example, no fancier from Duffel or Malines would go to Lier, even though Malines has more than a thousand organized fanciers. Pepermans from Zemst cannot avoid going to Lier five or six times every season, whether he wants to or not, and he manages to come out on top.

He can rely on the class of his pigeons. Of course, he trains them from a more southerly direction right from the beginning. Class is not enough. Even if his birds leave the drag behind them there are always other outstanding birds who are not put to shame by Pepermans' pigeons and can reach the same velocities. So Pepermans has to train his birds to take a more easterly route as they approach the southern part of the province of Brabant. And they pull it off! They follow a route approximately four miles east of that followed by the pigeons from Lier.

Single-up training tosses help, although I daresay the drag is the governing force. Nevertheless, I think we may say that everything helps.

How do our pigeons find their way home?

Any fancier who is faced with the same difficulties can draw conclusions from this example to help him solve his problems. It may be some consolation for him to know that many top fanciers in our country have to battle against the same difficulties.

It is all a question of landmarks, of points of recognition, which tell the pigeon at a certain point along the route to part with its fellows and continue on its own.

I mentioned the effect of the wind. I am not speaking about head or tail winds, which only influence velocities, but side winds which influence the direction the birds have to take. Depending on the strength of the side wind, they will deviate more or less from the direct route. And again it is the drag, the large mass of pigeons that are blown off course by the wind, which stamps its mark on the prize list, either favourably or unfavourably.

I wonder whether it is the wind alone which pushes the birds into a certain direction, on to a route which differs from the most direct way home?

To get an answer to this question we must turn to the fanciers from Waasland who enter in the Antwerp regional races. 'The sooner the birds are up the better for us,' they say. 'The later in the day the birds are liberated the worse off we are. We then stand little or no chance, unless the wind is in our favour. If it is against us, our birds don't even manage to get into the bottom end of the prize list! They are caught in the Antwerp flock.'

Why are the Waasland fanciers calling for an earlier liberation? They claim that the birds make for the coast if they are liberated in the early hours of the morning from a south-westerly race point. This means that the whole lot approach what is the correct route for the Waasland birds. Waasland lies west of Antwerp, i.e. towards the coast. I cannot disagree with the Waasland fanciers. The prize lists fully confirm their claims.

I would just like to add the following; some years ago French fanciers conducted extensive experiments which showed that the birds whose lofts had the greatest distance measurements reached the highest velocities and won the top prizes (on paper that is, when the prize list was worked out). All the birds had

How do our pigeons find their way home?

made for the coast, and for those that had the shortest distances to their lofts the additional mileage was proportionately greater.

The later in the day the birds are liberated, the less they are inclined to follow the coast. Why is there this strong desire to make for the coast in the early hours of the morning? I do not believe that a satisfactory answer to this problem has yet been found. Some say that the pigeons find more favourable winds and air currents along the coast; others that they do not like to fly with the sun shining straight into their eyes.

While it is true that facts cannot lie, I must admit that the phenomenon of westward deviation has so far defied explanation. So investigation must go on.

We know for a fact that pigeons are also guided by rivers and streams. They are helped not only by their sense of direction but by the appearance of the countryside, by landmarks and conspicuous features which serve as signposts.

Those who live on the heights of the Flemish Ardennes, around Oudenaarde and Ronse, will tell you that they hardly ever see a pigeon fly past. The large flocks follow the rivers Scheldt or Dender. Those living in between the two rivers only see the pigeons belonging to a few villages. Fanciers in these villages are always busy studying the direction of the wind and wondering whether they ought to race their birds with the clubs on the Scheldt or those on the Dender. I have been asked this question several times recently by these fanciers and have been able to go into the facts. I can vouch for their accuracy.

When scientists look into the problem of homing instinct they study things which are undoubtedly of interest to us too. Strange as it may sound though, they are not of prime importance.

Our main concern is not how our pigeons find their way home, but why. Instead of taking the shortest way home, they often deviate from the direct, the ideal route. But it is worth knowing to what extent we can make use of scientific findings in racing so that we can compete against our opponents with an equal chance and without a handicap.

We try to study the factors of drag, wind, race point, time of

How do our pigeons find their way home?

liberation and race route with its natural obstacles. We try to calculate our chances by allowing for all these factors, we try to exploit what may help and avoid what is detrimental.

Yet still we often see good birds, handicapped by certain circumstances, quite unreasonably beaten by other birds which have been favoured by the same circumstances. This is what one sporting journalist very rightly called the element of uncertainty in every sport.

Uncertainty is part of pigeon racing. This is why the theory of probability must be applied, and that is an art in itself.

A young fancier once asked me what the great and famous breeders were so busy discussing with each other all the time. Literally he said, 'I would like to be a little mouse and eavesdrop.'

The answer is very simple, they talk about past and future races, about the expectations of some and the past experiences of others. They discuss these points, trying to convince each other and at the same time pick each other's brains. A lot can be learned from them, especially by beginners, but also by older fanciers, who frequently go about their racing in a much too careless way.

Pigeon racing means more than simply going to the loft, putting a bird into a basket and then waiting to clock in the rubber ring. What happens before that is infinitely more important. But this does by no means sum up the whole business. Some thought on homing ability must not be left out of this book. It is a problem which has always attracted our interest and always will. Let's examine the question of how our pigeons find their way home, from a place they have never been before, where, despite their good eyesight, they can see nothing that is familiar to them from previous flights, where they know no landmarks, nothing which could serve as a signpost.

If young, untrained birds are sent on a long-distance race all but a very few will be lost. Older birds, trained over short distances from the loft and used to flying on short-distance races, will take longer than birds used to flying long distances,

How do our pigeons find their way home?

but most of them will return home. Of course, these examples do not apply to birds that fly with the drag, since they will get a measure of help from the trained birds.

The problem has kept scientists busy for years, for it does not apply only to racing pigeons. The problem of homing ability concerns many other animals. It applies equally in the case of migratory and non-migratory birds, bees, fish, even reptiles and butterflies. Among the many names we come across in books and periodicals dealing with homing ability some deserve a special mention. The names of the British scientist Dr. Matthews and the German Dr. Kramer and his school crop up again and again in the extensive literature on the subject.

No one would claim that the problem has been completely solved. This is proved by the reports published in recent times. It is, therefore, quite possible that in time everything which has been established so far will be supplemented by entirely new material.

It is beyond the scope of this book to quote every opinion ever voiced, every thesis ever put forward. I can say with a clear conscience that, by general agreement, orientation is based on two factors, the *clock* and the *sun*.

In *Bird Navigation* Dr. Matthews speaks of a kind of clock mechanism in birds, of sun-arc navigation, of using the sun as a compass. Dr. Gustav Kramer and his colleagues at the Max Planck Institute at Wilhelmshaven have gone into the questions and their findings roughly agree with Dr. Matthews, though I say 'roughly' only.

It is certain that pigeons must be able to see the sun to be able to depart, in the right direction, from the race point. The sun need not be blazing down from a cloudless sky. Even if the sky is overcast, or it is raining or slightly foggy, the birds will fly off as long as they can tell the position of the sun by a faint glow, a light patch behind the clouds or the fog. If the sun is overcast or only partly visible, orientation is certainly made more difficult, and velocities drop considerably. But experienced birds will not fail to get home. The sun is used as a compass, and like every compass it serves to indicate the direction.

How do our pigeons find their way home?

Why is it that pigeons, released on an international race in the South of France, whose home is to the north, fly off in a northerly direction? Why do they not fly off to the south?

Pigeons from Belgium and Britain strike almost due north. At the Channel coast the British birds cross the water and turn slightly west. The Belgian birds from Limbourg and Liège take a slightly more easterly route; their direction is north-northeast. The German birds take an even more easterly course. Why?

The fact is, that as the birds are liberated they note the position of the sun at the race point and compare it with the position of the sun at the home lofts, which they know. All birds see the sun in the same position at the moment they are released. But they take different routes northwards, depending on the position of the sun at home. As the day goes on so the position of the sun changes, because of the rotation of the earth.

The sun travels through the sky, from horizon to horizon, in an arc, rising in the east and setting in the west. The arc goes from the lowest point on the eastern horizon through the highest point at noon to the lowest point on the western horizon. This happens in the course of one day. We also know that in summer the sun is longer in the sky and rises higher than in winter. We say the days are longer or shorter. The further south we go the higher is the sun in the sky. The further we go north the lower is the arc it describes across the sky. In addition to this, the sun reaches its zenith (highest point) sooner in the east than in the west. All this means the sun is in a different position all the time, and the pigeon knows precisely what this position is at home.

We can come to the conclusion, therefore, that pigeons have a sense of time. If they did not they could not possibly tell the difference between the sun's position at the race point and that at the home loft at the same moment. I must emphasize this fact.

We have to admit, this is fantastic, truly fantastic.

Pigeons that are liberated in the South of France in the early hours of the morning and have to race north notice that the sun is higher in the sky than it would be at the same time at home.

How do our pigeons find their way home?

They choose their route to make good this difference. During the race the position of the sun changes all the time. The birds' sense of orientation, the 'internal clock', is ceaselessly at work. The sun compass is consulted and, if necessary, the flight direction changed. Our pigeons work like pilots with their modern instruments, who, by making calculations and taking radio bearings, can fix their course and if necessary change it. Does all this prove that the thesis of the 'internal clock' and the 'sun compass' is right?

Let us take a quick look at the honey bee. Over half a century ago the Swiss naturalist, August Forel, found that bees visited him only at breakfast to help themselves to the sweet things on the table. Those who have read something about the life of the honey bee will know that bees 'talk' to each other. A bee that has found something good returns to the hive and performs a dance which tells the other bees about the food and where it is to be found.

Through the pattern of the dance and the smell the bee has brought back from the feeding place, the other bees manage to find the right spot very quickly. But how do they find the way? What do they go by? And something else, why did the bees never visit Forel except in the morning? And why did they continue to come in the morning when, as an experiment, he had put out nothing sweet?

These experiments demonstrate without a doubt that a bee is capable of orientation and that it has a time sense. Forel called it 'time memory'.

H. von Buttle-Reepen noticed that bees visited a field of buckwheat some time in the morning because nectar was given off by the flowers only at that particular time. There wasn't a bee to be seen at any other time. This shows that the bees remembered when there was something to be had from the buckwheat flowers and when there wasn't, and it proves Forel's theory. We can indeed speak in terms of a time sense.

Now let's get back to pigeons.

Every fancier knows that on long-distance races hens stay

How do our pigeons find their way home?

longer on the wing in the evening and are up earlier in the morning of the second day than the cocks. We also know that hens stand less chance on short-distance races if liberation is postponed from the very early hours of the morning to later in the day. The fanciers say, 'It's too late, the hens are past their best.'

Why do hens fly later at night and continue the race earlier next morning? Maternal worries? Undoubtedly. This immediately raises the question why, if the liberation takes place later in the day, these maternal worries should have vanished by then.

I think we can assume that the hen, having a time sense, knows that her time to sit on the nest is from late afternoon to mid-morning on the following day, and that the cock takes over the incubation for the rest of the time. The fact that during the absence of one the other remains on the nest the whole time does not invalidate this theory.

Biologists studying the problem of homing ability and orientation in animals are investigating this question with great thoroughness. They carry out experiments and meet at scientific congresses to publish the results of their researches, and submit them for general criticism, hoping in this way to arrive at the correct solution.

I have spoken about this problem because I believe that it has a place in this book, but I have only outlined it very roughly; just enough to give fanciers an idea of the complexity of the question.

This, then, is the conclusion we have reached. We must accept that the birds use the sun as a compass. We must also accept the rather incredible idea that pigeons have an internal clock. They have a memory. They know the position of the sun in their home region at different times of the day and year and 'read' their clock as we read our wrist watches. It remains to be seen what more science can discover.

My personal opinion is that the present theory will possibly be supplemented in the future by some interesting facts. Perhaps the last word has not yet been spoken. But on the whole, the present theory on homing ability in pigeons should be accepted.

11

A look behind the scenes

Some of my colleagues on the pigeon racing press have said to me, justifiably, I must admit:

'You visit just about all the best lofts in the country. In your articles you have quoted the names of many top fanciers whose houses you treat practically as your own. You have followed the development of these lofts and you still do. Shouldn't you be able to tell us something more about them? All you do is give a few details here and there, but surely the ordinary man, the small breeder, would appreciate it most of all if you let him take a closer look at the lofts of your friends.'

Well then, I had better try to make up for my omissions in this book. But this will be no secret look at the great lofts; there are no secrets in pigeon racing. Anyone with this idea in his head has still got a lot to learn. He has never had the good fortune to own good pigeons or he would know that a crack bird flies without secret aids and remedies and that the fancier who experiments with his birds any in such way will ruin them.

Having said this, I will pass on some tips which, I hope, will help the average fancier. They are drawn from the experience of our top breeders, whose advice is always be wary of theories and on guard against advertising.

From many possibles, I have chosen the following breeders to talk about: Emile Matterne from Overhespen, Fons Van

A look behind the scenes

Elsacker from Loenhout, Louis Pepermans* from Zemst, and Jef Van Riel from Ekeren-Donk.

I have already mentioned Emile Matterne from Overhespen in the first chapter; now I want to say some more about this great fancier and his unusual method of loft management, which is by the so-called 'dry-droppings method'. Matterne did not decide on this method as a matter of principle; it arose from necessity.

Anyone who knows Matterne well knows that he is a teacher in a state school. His school is about 30 miles from Overhespen. He just hasn't the time to keep his lofts clean, to scrape and sweep them or clean and lime the nest bowls. Besides, he hasn't got only ten breeding pairs and a dozen widower cocks. He has quite a few more!

As I mentioned before, he only races on the difficult long-distance routes. Any pigeons which are not ready to go on these go on training races to gain experience for future years. So he has to have a fair number of pigeons, and they all need looking after. In the circumstances there is only one solution, the 'dry-droppings method'.

Not everyone can use this method in a way that suits the birds. There is one condition which cannot under any circumstances be dispensed with. *The lofts must be bone-dry*.

Anyone who cannot meet this condition must look for a different solution; scrape and sweep, or have someone do it for you if you have no time to do it yourself, and see that it is done thoroughly.

All of Matterne's lofts are bone-dry. The space his family needs for living rooms and bedrooms (and this is not inconsiderable with six growing children) is on the ground floor. Any part of the house that has to be reached by stairs and ladders is occupied by pigeons.

* This outstanding Belgian pigeon fancier, L. Pepermans, died suddenly from a heart attack on 19th August 1968. At the auction of his birds on 24th November and 1st December, all records were beaten by a long way. They sold for over 3 million Belgian francs with an average of over 11,000 francs – the 'Golden Hen' was a topper at the auction with 90,000 francs plus 20% for taxes. (J.A.)

A look behind the scenes

When I last visited Matterne it was a sunny day, but quite a strong wind was blowing. All the loft windows were wide open, so that the wind was free to blow in. 'How about draught?' I heard somebody say. There is no draught here, never. The birds can fly in and out of the windows as they please, but the individual lofts are completely self-contained inside. The wind can blow in through a window but has to leave again by the same window after having 'visited' every corner of the loft. Any pigeon that wants to visit a loft other than its own is free to do so. There are no notices saying 'Keep Out'! But when the bird wants to return to its own loft it must leave by the way it came in.

One loft was unoccupied that year. It had housed the yearlings the previous year and would do so again the following year. In that particular year the whole of the loft had been scrubbed, swept and limed. The wind was allowed to blow in and out unrestrictedly, day and night.

When you see the lofts housing the breeding and racing birds on the upper floor, at first you cannot believe your eyes, unless you have seen a loft run on the dry-droppings method before. All the loft floors are covered with several inches of dry droppings, and all the pigeons, young and old alike, walk over it with dry, clean feet. They fly in and out of the loft without taking any notice of visitors.

That day I had asked my wife to come along with me to Overhespen. I wanted her to see this spectacle. It can be quite amusing to watch the reactions of a house-proud woman who is used to going round with duster and mop an hour after she has put down her brush and pail. 'Come into the garden,' I said to her, 'and have a look at the breeding lofts there. There are quite a few pigeons in them. You will be amazed how clean they all are.'

The doctor had forbidden her to climb stairs, so she had to be shown the garden lofts. She threw up her hands in horror. Every pair of pigeons had a nest box with one or two nest bowls in it, but I only saw three that were occupied. All the other birds had

A look behind the scenes

made their nests on the floor, amid the droppings, adding straw to them.

'Look at this! Here is a bird sitting on her eggs and all round the nest are seven youngsters, just weaned. Obviously they are not her own.'

When feeding time comes round the young birds eat with the old ones. Those that are too young to look after themselves are fed by their parents or any old bird that happens to be handy. This is a society where there is no strife. Its members don't peck and fight each other, except when an old bird gets too close to some youngsters lying snugly in their nest and disturbs their peace. If this happens the youngsters peck and the old bird makes off in a hurry.

In one corner there was an orange box, about 15 to 20 inches high. It had straw and dry droppings in the bottom. A hen was sitting on her nest in one corner and opposite her two youngsters, about a fortnight to three weeks old.

Within the next week someone would have to lift these two out of the box and put them on the floor because they would not be able to leave it by themselves.

My wife was utterly amazed, 'I have never seen anything like it. He ought to charge people to see it. But how come I can't smell anything? And all the birds look so clean! There isn't a single dirty feather on any of them. Even their feet are spotless!' It really amazed us, as it had amazed many visitors before.

Whether we are for or against the dry-droppings method, it is certain that at Overhespen the pigeons are one hundred per cent healthy and very successful. The only difference between their way of life and that of wild pigeons is that they do not have to seek their own food and shelter but are given both.

Nobody can expect me to advocate the dry-droppings method. I am in favour of a thorough daily cleaning of the lofts, the nest boxes, the floors, in short everything which comes into contact with the droppings. I advise fresh drinking water with every feed, the daily cleaning of drinking fountains and the cleaning and liming of the nest bowls before use. I advocate the

A look behind the scenes

regular use of modern preparations to combat parasites. To put it in a nutshell: I like a spotlessly clean loft. But if somebody finds himself in Matterne's situation and can offer his birds a bone-dry loft then—and only then —would I advise him to try the dry-droppings method. I say 'try', for I don't think it can be made to work everywhere. It can go wrong, horribly, completely wrong.

Now a word about the small fancier. Small fanciers often complain that pigeon racing is too expensive. This may be true, but in most cases the trouble is lack of rational planning. Small fanciers keep too many pigeons; not all the pigeons in their loft are worth keeping. If this isn't the case the they don't race their birds as they should. They never send them out of sight of their own church spire and only race over the short distances, although I am convinced that their birds could win prizes beyond that. Let's, therefore, have a look at a small breeder with a 'classical system'. By small breeder I mean anyone who only has a limited number of pigeons in his loft. Small, but good. I would like to show you that a small loft can successfully compete with the bigger ones. Let's visit one of those small lofts.

Fons Van Elsacker lives at Loenhout on the Antwerp-Breda motorway, near the Dutch border. He is a carpenter and his work takes him away from home quite a bit. His wife is then left to feed the birds and look after them and give them the necessary exercise.

It is at least ten years since I was introduced to Van Elsacker by a friend in Malines from whom he wanted to buy some young birds. As usual, he had with him a basket with four of his own birds in it. He wanted to make sure that the birds he was going to buy were of the same type. When I saw these four birds I said, 'Vermeijen strain, aren't they?'

'How did you know?' Van Elsacker asked in surprise. 'You're right.' Quite frankly I didn't know. I had only guessed.

Like sheep, pigeons of the same colour all seem to look alike at first. Later, you notice details and individual characteristics and gradually you get to know them. How could I have guessed

A look behind the scenes

the strain of these birds? I knew birds belonging to the late Louis Vermeijen, once a colleague of mine on *De Duif*, and these four birds all showed characteristics of his strain. Their irises had an unusual shade of carmine red in them, and they had a 'saddle', i.e. the uniformly light-coloured feathers on their back were interspersed with a few dark ones. These are features you meet with occasionally. Like red or black feet in youngsters they have nothing to do with the quality of the strain.

So we got to know one another by chance, and ever since I have visited Van Elsacker regularly to advise him on selection and pairing up. Fons maintains that a stranger often detects faults that the fancier himself ignores, because he knows the pigeons and is only too eager to deceive himself. There is certainly some truth in that.

Van Elsacker set himself a difficult task. Small as the number of his pigeons was, he changed over from short-distance to long-distance racing, from short-distance racing in his club and neighbouring clubs to races from beyond Paris in the Antwerp Union, a venture which needed a good deal of ambition.

True, you can race very well in and around Loenhout, but the Union has always had a reputation for top-class racing. Fanciers who have raced well in their own clubs and clubs nearby have often been disappointed when they have tried their luck in the Antwerp Union. It collects the cream of Antwerp fanciers.

Well, I must admit that Van Elsacker's pigeons came from the best lofts, so he started off with top material. But any fancier with a small loft who wants to win prizes that count cannot afford not to race his hens. If he also sticks to the rule, 'Kill the good ones and only keep the outstanding ones', as Van Elsacker does, then he must be very strict in his selection. Strict selection means breeding many youngsters, for even in top lofts the percentage of really good young birds is very low.

In the first year only four old widow hens and five breeding pairs were left, the latter on probation. They were to be judged by their progeny, not the other way round. Selection continued

A look behind the scenes

throughout the year among everything from eggs to fully-moulted birds. Performance was taken into account. At the end of the year scarcely ten per cent of all the young birds were left. No youngsters that had the slightest flaw went into a basket. Only six of the young cocks were kept through the winter. As yearlings, they were trained on the natural system, mated to hens that raced on long distances.

The difference between this loft and many other Belgian ones lies in the fact that Van Elsacker hardly ever races cocks beyond the 180-mile stage, while his hens are never sent on anything less than that.

The hens are withdrawn from racing when they are four years old. Those that have already proved good breeders go into the breeding loft. This means keeping three or four young hens each year to pair up with the yearling cocks.

Young cocks are hardly ever trained beyond Paris. If the weather is bad they go no farther than Noyon (140 miles). Young hens are tested as far as Châteauroux (354 miles). Cocks are raced from the beginning of May till the middle of July. Young birds start at the end of June. Young and old hens go into the basket until the end of August, sometimes even the beginning of September, depending on the racing schedule and the progress of the moult; the young birds go on training tosses and the older ones on long-distance races. They have to work hard.

Van Elsacker enjoys racing on this system every year. The birds are not overworked because they are raced alternately. Their keenness in racing does not flag prematurely.

The fact that each season the long-distance hens are mated to six yearling cocks shows that Van Elsacker believes in pairing up on probation. No breeding pair, even in the breeding loft, stays together for longer then two years. Pairing on probation is the best way to find the ideal breeding pair. For pairing up, I repeat, is a gamble. The more combinations you have, the better your chances of success. The fact that Van Elsacker relies more on experiment than on professional know-how does not mean

A look behind the scenes

that he pays no attention to theory or experience. Anyone who has been in pigeon racing for many years knows only too well that he is frequently faced with surprises which make nonsense of well-planned and obvious combinations.

In most lofts it is quite usual to split up pairs and mate them to different birds the following season. Any pair which has produced poor offspring is separated. That is a rule, but any pair which has bred well is left together. There is one thing, though; a good breeding pair does not produce equally good offspring every year. There are bound to be bad years, and it is a fact that a good, old breeding cock is usually kept on year after year. It cannot be denied, however, that it is often better to replace the cock by a younger one with more fire.

As far as Van Elsacker's racing system is concerned, the widower cocks race on the classical system which everyone knows. The hens are sent to race towards the end of incubation time or with an egg just hatching, or sometimes when they are feeding young up to twelve days old. A close watch must be kept on every individual hen and its form.

With six hens sitting the fancier can send two or three hens to every long-distance race, as long as the races are held at fortnightly intervals. This makes it possible to send those hens that are in peak form.

The hens are raced on 'pseudo-widowhood', which means that the cocks stay on the nest during the day and the hen takes over from late afternoon until the following morning. It is mainly the cock, though, who takes over feeding the young, to give the hen a rest.

One July, Van Elsacker sent three hens to Châteauroux, duplicated into the provincial race. He won three prizes and the first series of two. The first nominated hen made fourteenth prize provincial out of 1,853 starters, and twelfth prize Union out of 748 starters. This brought in a total of 5,500 Belgian Francs (about £40 or $110) in prize money, which is not bad considering that the hens were competing against widower cocks. Nobody could say that this wasn't a splendid success.

A look behind the scenes

I would like to tell you how the hens were prepared for racing, for I saw it myself. Each hen has a youngster about twelve days old. She is left alone with the young bird, which lies in the nest bowl in the part of the nest box that is partitioned off. She can see it but not get at it. The hen is put into the basket, the youngster stays at home, unprotected so the hen thinks, since she has not seen the cock for some days.

All drinking fountains are removed from the loft. The hens are first fed Tasmanian maple peas. They fall on them greedily because they think their youngsters are hungry. There is enough food for some to be left over. The fancier is in no hurry and goes to visit the widower loft. When he comes back after some ten minutes the hens are given the basic mixture I described earlier. He waits until they have finished feeding. As before, they fly to where the drinking fountains should be, but they are not there; so they eat some more. When they will take no more of the mixture, they are given dari, followed by the classic seeds. Now the hens have had more than enough and are given plenty to drink. But they are not allowed to go near their young. They are put into a basket in a cool spot.

Now the cocks are let into the loft. They are given their full feed and have ample opportunity to feed their hungry youngsters. Shortly before it is time to take the hens to the club, the cocks are removed from the loft and the hens brought back. They descend once again on the drinking fountains, quench their thirst and are then allowed to feed their youngsters. Since these have been fed already, they take very little food. Now the hens are basketed again and taken to the club.

The hens go into the basket thinking that their youngsters are left behind without protection. Thus prepared, they have not dissipated their energies, they are well fed and are given some more to drink in the basket. Full of energy and spurred on by maternal instinct, they devote their full attention to racing home at top speed and stand a good chance against the widower cocks.

Experience has shown that this is so. The preparation hens

A look behind the scenes

need takes no more time and effort than the preparation of cocks. Like cocks, hens are sent out on an hour's exercise a day while the loft is closed. Racing hens over the difficult middle, half and long-distances is as profitable as racing cocks. It does not mean that the fancier has to keep a larger number of birds; in fact he can even get by with less. He can race longer, and breed without interruption from the best fliers.

Fons Van Elsacker is a straightforward man who knows what he wants from his birds and what he can expect from them. To him pigeon racing is a sport, a hobby, which gives him great pleasure. He does not only race hens over the long distances, for there are quite enough races in the Union anyway in which hens may compete on their own or be duplicated with widower cocks.

It is a characteristic of fanciers who send their hens on difficult races that they also send their best cocks. They can do better than their opponents who only race cocks. Why is that? Hens that do no good are got rid of, which means that these fanciers only breed from birds that have proved they possess exceptional racing qualities.

I have repeatedly been criticized by people who say that such stringent selection inevitably means that good hens are got rid of without being given a chance to show what they have in them. There can be no doubt that among the worst weeded out every year in the loft and by the basket there will be some good hens. On the other hand, it is quite certain that the birds left over will be no worse than these good ones. The number of pigeons in the loft remains the same, but the average quality improves, so that it is quite clearly a case of 'Get rid of the good ones and keep the best.'

Van Elsacker has never yet finished a season without a nice credit balance. Apart from that, he always has a few good, selected birds he can use to help out a fancier friend or acquaintance who has done less well. He also manages to donate pigeons to many charity shows and thus helps to fill the kitty and give visitors the opportunity of buying something good from a small loft.

A look behind the scenes

Any modest fancier with a small loft can learn from this example. Van Elsacker has reached a high standard with just a few pigeons, the minimum of expense and time. And he enjoys the sport very much, too.

Now let us turn to the third man in the group, Louis Pepermans at Zemst. We have seen how Van Elsacker prepares his hens before a race. Now we will take a look at how thoughtfully Pepermans cares for his birds when they come back from a race. He has no time for people who neglect their pigeons when they return from a difficult race.

'I cannot understand', he says, 'why they don't use their common sense.' And then he tells of an incident, 'I once watched the finish of an important cycle race on television. Journalists and reporters were waiting for the winner at the finishing line, and he had scarcely arrived when they asked him to step in front of the microphone. He was covered in dirt and dripping wet because it had been raining during the race, but nobody thought of putting a coat or a blanket round the shoulders of the exhausted man to prevent him catching pneumonia. A pigeon fancier who sat beside me commented quite rightly that such behaviour was unpardonable. And yet he happened to be one of the very fanciers who throw a handful of food at their pigeons when they return and then dash down to the club to satisfy their curiosity about how the birds have done.'

Like people who take part in a sport, pigeons are athletes too. Both men and birds have to be treated well and cared for after a race.

On the morning of a race, Louis Pepermans makes a study of all the factors likely to influence the performance of his pigeons and their degree of tiredness, such as distance, temperature, wind direction, wind strength, time spent in the basket, means of travel (train, road, air), time of liberation, etc. When the birds return, he compares his calculations with the actual performance of every bird. The result decides how long each hen may stay with her cock. It also determines the time at which the cock is given its second feed.

A look behind the scenes

The first feed, together with a drink, awaits the cock in his nest box. The water has been brought to loft temperature by filling the fountains the day before the race. I must emphasize that Louis uses only pure water, straight from the tap, with no glucose, sugar or honey added.

When Louis talks about pigeons, his main concern is always feeding the birds after a race. He brings up again and again an aspect which most fanciers ignore: the bird that wins a top prize is usually less tired than the one that returns late, or at least later. The latter has been on the wing longer since it took longer to get back to the loft. It has also had a more difficult race because it has had to work harder. This bird deserves special care by the fancier. Pepermans can speak with authority, for he always enters a team in which every single bird is capable of winning the first prize. If any of them don't return among the leaders, it means that they have had difficulties beyond their control or that they were not in peak form. Pepermans gives particular attention to latecomers to make sure that they do better in the next race. What chance would they stand of doing better if they were not given special treatment to bring them back into peak form?

It is usual for a bird which returns fresh and unspent to attend first to its mate, waiting in the closed half of the nest box. Only then will it quench its thirst and take some food. A bird which is tired will normally (I am not saying *necessarily*) think of drink and food first. The difference in behaviour is a clue to the degree of tiredness in the bird.

The hen sitting in the closed nest box has had nothing to eat in advance and will share the slim meal with the cock. By 'slim' I mean a light meal consisting of equal parts of wheat, barley, dari, paddy rice, sunflower seeds and one or two grains of maize. The birds only take enough to satisfy the worst of their hunger. They have done heavy work; their bodies are tired and have to rest. It would not be sensible to burden their digestive organs with a heavy diet.

There is another mistake many fanciers are guilty of. They

A look behind the scenes

think that the more difficult the race was the longer the hen should be allowed to stay with the cock. This is quite wrong. The pair get the promised contact with one another, and that is enough. The hen, who has not been away from home, is eager to be courted and will pester the cock more than is good for him. She will prevent him from getting the rest he needs, and this must not be allowed to happen under any circumstances.

When it is time to take the clock down to the club, Pepermans tells a member of his family at what time, to the minute, each hen has to go back into her own loft. After a 300-mile race, the times the pairs are allowed to stay together vary from a quarter to half an hour. The last ones home get about ten minutes. Always remember, the last home are the most tired and so must be given the least time.

A bird which comes home too late to win a prize must nevertheless find his hen waiting for him in the nest box. Animals never pretend. If a bird is late it simply could not do better on that occasion; it would not do to discourage it, for every domestic pet, be it a dog, cat, canary or pigeon, looks forward to good treatment and a kind word from its master. If it doesn't get it, it feels neglected and unhappy. If a pigeon feels lonely, its performance in the next race is bound to suffer.

When all the hens have left the widower loft, the nest boxes are opened and the cocks all descend to the floor where they drink from the communal drinking fountain. They take some grit and the odd small seed, but there should not be more than 1 gram of this per bird. Pepermans adds a few breadcrumbs to the seed mixture I have already described.

When do the birds get their second meal? This usually happens at about 5 o'clock in the afternoon if they have returned, as is usual, between 11 a.m. and 1 p.m. The feed is the same again, a light mixture, but this time there is plenty of it. Not too much, though, for the birds must not be overfed, since this would not allow their bodies to rest properly.

When do the birds go back on to the heavy mixture? This depends on how difficult the race was, whether any of the birds

A look behind the scenes

need a week's rest, and what race is scheduled for the following week. The answers to these questions determine, for each bird separately, the date of the change-over to the basic mixture. A bird that is sent again the following Sunday will be given the heavy mixture on Tuesday morning or evening. A bird that is given a week's rest will be fed the basic mixture on the Saturday.

All birds must be fit to race again by the next week. Any bird that isn't can be got rid of without a qualm, unless the race was a difficult long-distance one.

Experience has shown that competition among fanciers is extremely keen and that large prizes can be won or lost by mere decimal points of velocity. Many fanciers, therefore, go in for team racing. This is Pepermans' so-called secret, and he chalks up his wins Sunday after Sunday. Of course, it is not a secret at all, for I have mentioned it several times in my articles. Any observant fancier can discover it for himself from the ring numbers in the prize lists. He can see which pigeons have been racing and which have not.

Everything Pepermans does in pigeon racing, he tries to do exactly right. It is interesting to know how he feeds his birds and why. When the birds are back to the normal mixture each gets his helping in his nest box. All get a generous helping, which means more than enough. In this way they can choose. If they take all the legumes and leave the maize (which is usual for most of them on Tuesday and sometimes even Thursday) Pepermans knows that the restoration of muscle tissue is not yet complete. As soon as a bird leaves some of the legumes he is on the way to new racing fitness. He then takes mainly maize and other non-protein seeds. If muscle tissue has been burnt it must be replaced. For this, mainly protein is needed. Only when the repairs have been completed is glycogen stored and reserves built up.

When the birds have finished feeding in their nest boxes, all the food that is left over is collected and put into the communal trough. Any bird that has not had enough legumes can come and get them now, and the same goes for maize. In this way they all get what they need, and none of the food is wasted.

A look behind the scenes

It is definitely wrong to give birds a large helping of mixed food on their return from a race. Even a light feed contains some protein. But this is not what the birds need most of all when they return; what they need is rest. They are overheated and tired. They need to take it easy, and they must be given plenty of time to recover. No bird can race consistently for three months if its owner tries to keep it in peak form all the time. Once the birds are home, they are given rest and relaxation and are then gradually brought back into peak form through a heavier diet.

Before I conclude this report on the Pepermans' loft I would like to mention something which many readers will call a fancier's whim. But read what I have to say first and judge afterwards.

Pepermans is always talking to his pigeons. It has happened that fancier friends of Pepermans have waited in his garden for what they thought were visitors to come down from the loft for they heard voices there. But there were no visitors. They had been fooled by Pepermans talking to his pigeons.

You don't agree with him? You think that pigeons do not understand the language of men? Ask yourself if a small baby understands his mother, who talks to him incessantly. What she says apparently makes no sense, pet names and cooing noises, but the child starts to gurgle and laugh. It is not the words but the sound of the voice which tells the child and the pigeon that someone takes an interest, someone cares.

Pepermans' pigeons are not shy, but they do not like being handled. He only handles them if it is absolutely necessary, and then he does it with the utmost gentleness. No rough handling! that is his motto. His pigeons are wrigglers; they always try to get free from the hand that holds them. They are nervous birds, fighting birds, and very often the little stick has to come into action when they get too lively. Two or three stern taps on the floor and they all stop and pay attention.

If Pepermans wants to show anyone a bird or examine it more closely, he drives it into its nest box, slowly and deliberately,

A look behind the scenes

in slow motion, so to speak, talking to it nicely all the time. Only when it is inside the box does he get hold of it.

There are hardly any widower cocks in his loft who pitch straight through the window into their nest box. Usually they sit down on the window-sill first, cooing and turning, so that Mrs. Pepermans, who is always in the loft when the birds return, has to go out on to the balcony through another door and shoo the bird in. The cock does this although he knows that his hen is waiting impatiently in the box.

'One shouldn't exaggerate the attraction of the hen,' says Pepermans. 'What do my young, unmated cocks do? I know that they are drawn as much to my wife and myself as to a hen.' Pigeons know very well who their friends are, who tames the troublemakers and protects the peaceful.

A shy bird which sounds the alarm at the slightest provocation can ruin the whole loft. But where the birds have a close relationship with their owner a happy atmosphere prevails. This is how it should be; anything else has a detrimental effect on racing performance. Some lofts have never lost a bird. After a bad race, exhausted birds reach home after days or weeks. If they had not had a good home they would have given up the search and found another loft.

I would like to repeat once more that we could benefit from studying the masters of our sport.

One thing I must not forget. It is a so-called trick which has proved very useful at Zemst. Occasionally a hen loses interest in her cock or vice versa. This must not be allowed to happen, for it is generally recognized that a passionate hen makes a good racing cock, and that this system only works if there is perfect harmony between the two partners.

The ties usually slacken towards the end of the season and performance suffers. The remedy is to give the cock a young hen, an early-bred hen of the same year, preferably one which is not yet mated but is obviously interested in the opposite sex. Immediately, the cock will be on top of the world again. Pigeons, especially cocks, are not very particular when it comes to

A look behind the scenes

conjugal loyalty. This foible in both partners can be exploited to improve their performance.

The Frans Huyskens-Jef Van Riel partnership was dissolved in 1957. It was founded in 1945 and before long baffled the entire pigeon world at home and abroad by its continual success. Frans Huyskens had been under medical treatment for some time. When a heart specialist insisted that Jef Van Riel must withdraw from the sport for good, the whole loft was sold by auction in Brussels and Antwerp on two Sundays. The sale attracted a vast number of fanciers from all over the world and it fetched a record sum. The large majority of original Huyskens-Van Riel birds are now in Dr. Whitney's loft in the United States.

Huyskens has withdrawn from pigeon racing altogether. Jef has recently given his lofts to his son-in-law and is passing his know-how on to him to make sure that he follows in his footsteps. In Belgium—and abroad—pigeon racing is never discussed without the names of Huyskens and Van Riel being mentioned. Some say that Jef Van Riel beats them all when it comes to getting out of a pigeon all it's capable of.

One of the main features of any truly great man, no matter in which field, seems to be modesty. Van Rief does not talk much. It has been said that he would rather bite off his tongue than reveal a secret. I cannot let this go unchallenged. Although Jef is very quiet, he has never, either in the course of conversation or in special interviews, failed to reply to my questions. He has never been intolerant in his replies. He has always told what he considered to be the truth and added examples from his own experience. And he has always ended up by saying, 'But then who knows anything about a pigeon?'

I have said already that a pigeon is an enigma, a question mark on wings. Jef thought that was a very good definition.

The principles which guided Van Riel can be defined in a few words; true art is simple art, and this goes for pigeon racing, too. His motto is 'back to nature'. Be merciless in getting rid of any bird that is not 100 per cent healthy. As for the rest, give them a

A look behind the scenes

chance. Try to get to know the character and peculiarities of every bird and you will realize that you will never know everything there is to know about a pigeon. Keep only birds that are top performers; pigeons of average quality are legion.

No doubt you would like to know in more detail how the loft was run. Huyskens-Van Riel followed no particular system for breeding, but they attached great importance to type, quality and performance of the birds, which means they worked towards genetic uniformity.

I know of an exceptional cock who produced good offspring with several hens. This cock had a grandson who resembled him closely in type, performance and breeding value. The grandson had been sired by a half-brother, mated to a half-sister. When I asked why they did not continue on a system which had proved so extraordinarily successful in this case they promptly replied,

'We have no time for experiments. There are other pairs which produced very good offspring, too. It is easy to see that such attempts at close inbreeding do not stand much chance of success, unless you have two virtually perfect pigeons. And where would you find those?'

Nieces and nephews, however, were paired up quite frequently. I would like to refer back to Chapter Two, where I mentioned *Jonge Bliksem*, bred from *Bliksem* and *Sproet*, who were nephew and niece. It was through a hen bred by *Jonge Bliksem* that I got to know Dr. Whitney. He regarded that hen as the corner-stone of his loft.

When Van Riel was still racing on the natural system, he paired his birds differently each year. He had many fewer birds then and had to rely on trial and error to find the best pair. Widower birds can easily be discouraged by having their old partner taken away. They are only given a younger partner if their keenness lapses, if the ties between the two partners have become looser. What conclusion can we draw from this?

It is preferable if cocks which are used exclusively for breeding are given a new mate every year, or at least every two years. As

A look behind the scenes

far as widower cocks are concerned, it is advisable to watch the relationship between the partners.

Jef Van Riel claims that you can breed perfectly well from widower cocks but that there is, nevertheless, a difference between their young and those from the breeding loft. He says, 'You cannot breed solely from widower birds. Treat and look after the widow hen as well as you like, the system is still unnatural. Nature will not be mocked; she will take her revenge. What you gain by widowerhood you lose in breeding. This is Louis Pepermans' gospel. He gives his widower cocks a young hen before the season. As soon as the season gets under way they are given their old partners back. When the season is finished, they are once again given a young hen with a view to late-bred youngsters. Breeding from yearlings yields a larger percentage of good youngsters than breeding from old birds. The yearlings have more vitality and fire and have not yet had to do any hard work which can occasionally do some harm to the body, although the damage cannot be detected with the naked eye.'

Van Riel advises all beginners to race on the natural system. It is more interesting than the widowerhood system. It requires more ability and know-how and is more instructive. Not everybody knows the ins and outs of the natural system as well as he should. Widowerhood, on the other hand, requires no special knowledge.

Fanciers (the older ones included) would be well advised to leave an interval of ten days between rounds of youngsters. This gives the birds a rest and a chance to recover, more or less. It ensures their continued interest in racing. It also makes a difference to the young birds. It is hardly necessary to have a break between the first and second rounds, but certainly between subsequent ones. If the partners do not see one another for several days the attraction grows. The fire of love burns brighter, and this is what matters.

Huyskens-Van Riel have occasionally tried winter-bred youngsters, but only with great reluctance, when the date of

A look behind the scenes

the championships left them no choice. From confidential conversations with top-class breeders, I have learned that years of experience have shown youngsters hatched in April or May to be vastly preferable to winter-bred youngsters. The old birds, too, show the effects of winter breeding, slight though these effects may be.

What is there to be said about breeding from brothers of champion birds, who do not themselves perform well? Huyskens-Van Riel have never tried this. They leave it to the smaller breeders who have only a limited number of birds and have to make a virtue of necessity. If one of two nest brothers is a good flier and the other does not come up to standard, why should the latter be given a chance of breeding? The De Donk team only bred from champion pigeons. Again and again the best young birds were bred from top winners and the sisters and daughters of these birds.

As examples, I should like to refer to *Late Bange*, *Bliksem*, *Grote Lichte* and *Wittekop*. When it came to cross-breeding, Huyskens-Van Riel were always very particular in their choice of material. Considering the large number of pigeons they kept, they introduced very little new blood to their loft. But wherever there were good birds for sale at a public auction they paid any price for the bird that took their fancy. They had to have it. They also exchanged birds with friends they could trust. The best was only just good enough for them. Their scheme was the eternal cycle of cross-breeding, selection, back-mating, selection, etc., etc.

The thing I noticed again and again with Huyskens-Van Riel was their method of feeding. They fed each variety of grain separately to old and young birds, except for the breeding birds whose troughs were always full. As the food went, so it was replaced. Both young and old birds started off with tic beans until they didn't want any more. Then they were given peas, tares, maize, wheat etc., in that order.

Van Riel believed that this method of feeding had three justifications. It ensures that the feed is not unbalanced. It is

A look behind the scenes

easy to control the correct proportion of protein, carbohydrates and fats. A bird shows by the amount of legumes it eats how much of its reserves it has spent and needs to rebuild. At the same time, the birds show if they have a preference for one or another sort of grain.

The food requirements of a pigeon are determined by the task it has to perform (i.e. racing or breeding), by its current performance, by the amount of work it is required to do on a race, by the season, the temperature and many other factors.

Van Riel says that fanciers pay far too little attention to this problem; they should consider the detailed research that goes into the diet of athletes in all types of sport. Nor is the average fancier sufficiently concerned about the quality of the food. He must try to tell from his birds' droppings whether the food is sound. Even men who know something about grains and seeds can be taken in unless they examine the droppings thoroughly each day. The fancier who feeds all types of grain in one mixture cannot possibly know whether the feed suits all his pigeons, i.e. whether every bird gets enough of everything. I must mention, though, that certain birds have a preference for one or other type of grain. Some don't like beans but will eat more peas or tares instead.

Throughout all this it must never be forgotten that maize must be the main part of the diet. Maize is to a pigeon as bread is to man. Other feeds are just side dishes. If the fancier keeps this in mind he will not make the mistake of feeding his birds too heavy a diet, giving them too many legumes which overwork the liver and make the breast flesh take on a blue tinge instead of its normal pink colour. He will also prevent the physical discomfort and illness which are the inevitable result. The worst sin, however, is to give too generous a helping of the small seeds, the titbits. They should only be given to the birds after the morning feed, as a treat. In the Huyskens-Van Riel loft this 'dessert' was made up of equal parts of canary seed, linseed, hempseed, sunflower seed and chopped oats and the maximum fed to each bird was one level teaspoonful. Anything

A look behind the scenes

in excess of this is like poison. During breeding, the birds were hand-fed and feeding stopped as soon as they turned to the drinking troughs. This prevented them putting on fat. When they had ten to twelve-day old youngsters in the nest, they were given an additional helping of legumes.

Weaned youngsters were given each sort of grain separately, like the old birds. After a race the birds were allowed to fill up on a light diet: maize, wheat, barley. Depending on the circumstances, a heavier diet was introduced according to plan to get the birds back into form more or less quickly. The classic method is to feed a light diet that does not burden the body to suppress form, and a heavier diet to induce form and take the bird to its peak.

Finally, I must stress one point yet again: the pigeons' droppings, which must be yellowish brown in colour, indicate the proportion of maize fed and show the quality of the grain. In the lofts of the Cattrysse brothers there is maize on the floor all day long. When the next feed is due it is swept up and taken down to the hens and subsequently replaced by fresh maize. The Cattrysse brothers compete in difficult long distance races.

At the Huyskens-Van Riel loft at Ekeren-Donk, I have watched pigeons returning from Cormeilles (196 miles), which is just within the short-distance limit, and from St. Vinvent and Barcelona. They used to put on a spurt over the last few yards. Spectators kept asking themselves how it was possible that after the strains of a race the birds could approach at such speed. 'They are killing themselves,' they used to say. Frans Huyskens simply said, 'Ours are willing pigeons. This means that they do exactly what we want them to.'

I will put it another and more accurate way. The birds possess a quality which cannot be detected by the hand and eye. Only the basket can tell. The French say they are *mordant*, a word derived from *mordre* meaning 'to bite'. These birds bite; they are fighters. Two of the Huyskens-Van Riel birds once arrived home from a long-distance race almost simultaneously. Within seconds of each other they pitched on the alighting board and in

A look behind the scenes

their fury immediately started to attack each other with beaks and wings. They were still at it on the loft floor so hard that they could be picked up without them even noticing it.

Many have been tempted to ask, 'What is it they give their birds? How do they do it?' The question is best answered by a counter-question, 'What is it that you do and give to your pigeons which is different from what they do and give to theirs?'

For years I have been a regular visitor at Ekeren-Donk and at the lofts of many other Belgian champions. In the Huyskens-Van Riel loft you find water from the pump with nothing *ever* added to it. There are also several small troughs of grit standing around. Grit is given in small quantities and frequently renewed. If the birds are given large quantities of it they take hardly any on the second day. They want it fresh, that's all.

Huyskens-Van Riel stuck to food and water. 'Leave it at that,' they said, 'or things may go wrong.' This is the exact advice they have given visitors over and over again. Many fanciers came to buy a few eggs or a young bird. They thought they were entitled to be told some more, to be given a few useful hints. Well, they always got them, but they were not always satisfied. Some were even disappointed. 'Getting out of a pigeon what's in it?' The difference between a teacher in front of a class and a fancier with his pigeons in his loft is very slight. Both have to deal with a group in which each individual differs from the next. Each one has a different character, and if you think you have found two exactly alike you are utterly wrong. There are always shades and variations which have to be taken into consideration. The difference between children and pigeons is that children can put on an act. They can pretend to be different from what they really are. But pigeons are without guile. Animals don't pretend.

To give its best a pigeon must first of all be healthy. As well as this, the fancier must know the bird inside out. Pigeons do not differ from each other so much in their normal activities, their daily behaviour, but when they are in form a considerable change from normal behaviour can be detected in most birds.

A look behind the scenes

The fancier wonders what it all means. He is faced with a puzzle which is often only solved when the bird has put up an exceptional performance. Then he understands.

The fancier who uses all his senses, who has eyes and ears for everything that's going on in the loft, who wants to, and in fact does, get to know his pigeons, is usually helped by chance. I would like to give a few more examples.

Huyskens-Van Riel once built a new loft next to the old ones. It was not quite finished and all the windows had been left wide open to let the warm summer air in and help it dry. When the widower cocks were called in after their evening exercise not a bird appeared. The whole bunch had gone into the new loft, and every bird had found a place for himself. In the old loft the annual newcomers had always been allocated the nest boxes which had become vacant. They had had no choice, but now they were able to choose.

The following Sunday was a resounding success. The birds won prizes as never before. When the new loft was finished each bird was given a free choice. Wouldn't you say this gave the birds an uplift in their monotonous lives as widowers?

If some nest boxes in your loft have become vacant because, for one reason or other, their occupants have disappeared, and the time has come to house new birds in them, lock all the old occupants of the loft into their nest boxes and let the young ones choose, even if a fight breaks out. You will always benefit from this practice. A man who has to live in a house he doesn't like will not be happy there, nor will he do his best work. Like man, like pigeon.

If a fancier knows a bird, its habits and behaviour, he can avoid anything that might hinder form and at the same time do everything to help form. It is not easy to describe form in precise words, but from my talks with Jef Van Riel and from personal experience I think I can formulate the following rule: a pigeon is coming into form when its behaviour is noticeably different from normal.

In a previous chapter I talked about signs indicating form in

A look behind the scenes

general. I want now to give examples of particular cases where the fancier must either help to bring out form or let it develop by itself without hindering it in any way.

Your pigeons lie casually on one wing to take a nap. They always lie with their heads towards the window and the light. Suddenly one of them lies with its tail towards the window. With its head tucked beteeen its shoulders it sits in the farthest corner of the nest box. This is what my *Dark 640* at Puurs used to do. A bird has left is nest box and withdrawn to a quiet corner on the floor. Another one, usually sitting quietly in its place, runs all over the floor busily searching for feathers and straws and carrying them to its nest box. Yet another tries to get into the closed-off nest box belonging to a bird that has not returned from the last race. Or a bird comes right up to you as you enter the loft. It follows you round, stopping whenever you stop, pecking at your shoe-laces. He is trying to tell you that he needs something. He is begging from you.

Your pigeons have cold feet when you put them into the basket. No sign of form. When you take them out at the club to have them marked for the race you feel their feet glowing. Their bodies seem smaller and lighter. The birds lie in the basket and 'moan'. The birds are as quiet as mice in the basket. But when you want to take them out at the club you have to be quick or some would get away. Quiet birds start a fight with any pigeon that happens to be near them as soon as they are inside the race panniers. Nervous pigeons bring up their last meal while they are in the basket. You don't notice it until you take them out at the club.

I could quote many more examples. Every fancier will have experienced one or the other himself. The secret of success is to get to know the peculiarities of each bird and encourage any unusual behaviour.

My *Dark 640* always had a little board put into his nest box during morning exercise on basketing day to help him take a quiet nap in his corner.

It all boils down to being a born fancier, to having a gift for it. What gift?—an eye for a pigeon, the ability to see something

A look behind the scenes

which the next man misses; the ability to see something at once that others take days to work out.

Jef Van Riel's secret is no secret. It is his exceptional ability, his expert knowledge, his natural talent, combined with a keen eye and a cool head that have protected him from all the mistakes which could have hindered his success.

For this reason, neither he nor any other critically observant person will ever cease to regard the pigeon as an enigma. We never stop learning. Jef Van Riel was fully aware of this; but we, the large majority of fanciers, do not seem to know it, or deliberately ignore it. This is why Jef was called the only fancier to 'get out of a pigeon what's in it'.

Jef Van Riel reached enviable heights in pigeon racing, but he never put on airs. This modesty is what made him so popular with everyone.

12
And finally, a look at Fabry

In writing this book, my one aim was to be honest and impartial. Not everybody will agree with me on all points, nor is this necessary. Remember what I have said several times: 'Theories are words; facts are real and either contradict or confirm the theories.' It is for this reason that I have given so many examples and quoted so many facts. I may not have removed all doubts, but I hope I have provided guides to further thought.

I have recently been involved in a number of discussions on small pigeons versus large ones, on persistent close inbreeding versus inbreeding interspersed with cross-breeding, on the old strains which are said to exist and indeed prevail to this day, on the proportion of legumes in feeding mixtures and various other topics. I will therefore add a few more pages which might give you some food for thought.

One of the outstanding lofts in the country is that of G. and V. Fabry at Liège. This loft has been so successful over the past few years that everyone describes it as fantastic. One of my relatives at Liège put it in a nutshell: 'They have won just about everything here.'

In the following pages I should like to say a few words about the Fabry strain, which I personally regard as the most consistent Belgian strain of the past half-century. It has always been out in front, without a single setback, over all distances and against the toughest competition we have in Belgium. Not a single other strain has persisted for half a century with unfailing strength.

And finally, a look at Fabry

Some years ago, Fabry junior showed me some pigeons of his strain which were about to be sold. The birds were above average in size. They could have been called large. Looking through the list of birds bought by the Fabrys I found that they all came from lofts that keep medium, even small birds. You can draw your own conclusions from this.

Do they practice persistent, close inbreeding? Not Fabry! I gathered this from two separate loft reports. To illustrate the point I should like to quote the following passage from a letter by Georges Fabry:

'As you quite rightly say, foreigners make fools of themselves talking about pure strains which probably never existed. People dare to speak of pure Hansenne strain—ridiculous! I had the chance to take a look at the sale catalogue when Hansenne's loft was sold by auction after his death. Felix Gigot, who had been entrusted with the auction, wrote that the Hansenne strain had been evolved by inbreeding from close relations, which meant that it was pure. One look at the catalogue disproved this claim.

'Then there is talk of pure Wegge-pigeons. Explaining to me how he managed to maintain his position as one of the most successful Belgian fanciers, Karel Wegge showed me his wallet and remarked that he never hesitated to pay a good price for a good pigeon which might improve his strain.

'I cannot believe the claims of successful fanciers who say they have never introduced new blood into their lofts.'

The pharmacist Georges Fabry, now in his eighties, did precisely what all breeders of the old Belgian strains did. He drew on theory (science) and his own considerable experience (facts) to climb to the pinnacle of fame in twentieth-century pigeon racing. His son Victor has had plenty of opportunity to show that he is a worthy successor to his famous father. Anyone who doubts me should look at the prize lists of the past few years.

Where did the Fabrys get the birds to improve their strain? Most of them were descendants of their own pigeons in other

And finally, a look at Fabry

fanciers' lofts, but there were also some birds from top lofts which were entirely unrelated.

I will quote just a few names. They started with Hansenne-pigeons from Verviers and pigeons from Van de Velde at Oudenburg. Then they introduced Baclene-Henin, Havenith-De Feyter, Paul Sion, Bricoux and Duray, Van Bruaene (Lauwe), Jos. Van den Bosch (Berlaar) and De Scheemaker Bros. From De Somer (Turnhout) they got a grand-daughter of *Zotteke* and *Sture* (The Surly One) by Huyskens-Van Riel, the first two birds home in the 1949 St. Vinvent race for the province of Liège. They also bought from Leopold Collard (Louvain), Marissen (Oelegem), Trivier (Liège) and De Botselier (Okegem). Later they introduced Pepermans too. The most successful of Fabrys' pigeons came from cross-breeds, as the reports prove. Later they were back-mated to distant relations.

There is too much boasting among present-day fanciers about old strains which serve as models. I challenge the supporters of persistent, close inbreeding to practice what they preach. Close scrutiny leads to the conclusion that breeders in the past did exactly what we do today—inbreeding, selecting, cross-breeding, selecting, back-mating . . . and start all over again.

We are apt to forget that competition is much keener today. There are more people in the sport. In the past, racing was done on a system which was familiar only to the initiated. This put the ordinary man in the street at a considerable disadvantage. I say this with the greatest respect for the great names of the past.

Let's have a look at the Fabrys' feeding. It varies from period to period and passes almost imperceptibly from one diet to another. These are their mixtures, and I would particularly like to draw the reader's attention to the percentage of legumes throughout the year:

Winter Mixture: 50 per cent barley, 20 per cent wheat, 20 per cent maize, 10 per cent peas, tares or beans.

Breeding Mixture: 20 per cent wheat, 30 per cent maize, 30 per cent beans, peas or tares, 10 per cent dari, 5 per cent sunflower seeds, 5 per cent barley.

And finally, a look at Fabry

Racing Mixture: 15 per cent wheat, 40 per cent maize, 30 per cent beans, peas or tares, 10 per cent dari, 5 per cent sunflower seeds, and, as a treat two or three days prior to basketing, a little hemp seed.

Moult Mixture: 15 per cent barley, 25 per cent maize, 25 per cent wheat, 5 per cent sunflower seeds, 5 per cent hemp seed, 25 per cent peas or beans.

In conclusion I should like to give a few hints. The stock birds are paired up around the 15th of February, the two or three-year old racers around the 15th of March, the yearlings around the 15th of April. The racers incubate for 10 days and never breed before the season. After the racing season all widowers rear two young birds and then incubate for another ten days, after which the sexes are separated.

What qualities are required of breeding cocks? Racing success, vitality, a powerful build, a strong rump, good balance. And of breeding hens? Good pedigree, plus the same qualities as the cocks. The young birds are trained to about 90 miles. This is done without preparation and no importance is attached to the results.

A reporter on *De Duivenbode* (Deerlijk) once compared loft management at Fabry's and Pepermans'; the differences were so small that he was amazed at the similarity between these two top lofts, whose owners knew each other only by name and did not meet in person until September 1963, and my own observations, made later, completely confirmed his findings.